Lifeline
BIOGRAPHIES

■■■■

TIM BERNERS-LEE
Inventor of the World Wide Web

by Stephanie Sammartino McPherson

Twenty-First Century Books · Minneapolis

FOR MY HUSBAND, RICHARD, WITH LOVE AND THANKS

Twenty-First Century Books
A division of Lerner Publishing Group, Inc.
241 First Avenue North
Minneapolis, MN 55401 U.S.A.

Website address: www.lernerbooks.com

Library of Congress Cataloging-in-Publication Data

McPherson, Stephanie Sammartino.
    Tim Berners-Lee : inventor of the World Wide Web / by Stephanie Sammartino McPherson.
       p.   cm. — (USA TODAY lifeline biographies)
    Includes bibliographical references and index.
    ISBN 978–0–8225–7273–2 (lib. bdg. : alk. paper)
    1. Berners-Lee, Tim—Juvenile literature. 2. World Wide Web—History—Juvenile literature. 3. Computer scientists—Great Britain—Biography—Juvenile literature. 4. Telecommunications engineers—Great Britain—Biography—Juvenile literature. I. Title.
TK5102.56.B47M38 2010
004.092—dc22 [B]   2008050719

Manufactured in the United States of America
1 2 3 4 5 6 – PA – 15 14 13 12 11 10

R0422865030

USA TODAY Lifeline BIOGRAPHIES

Conference speaker: Tim Berners-Lee speaks at the Fourth International World Wide Web Conference in Boston, Massachusetts, in 1995.

A New Era

Timothy Berners-Lee stood onstage and gazed at a sea of excited faces. Every seat in the auditorium was taken, and many people had been turned away. Those who could not get tickets sent frantic e-mails. "I must be there," a typical message might read. "I don't need food. I don't need lodging. I'll sit on the steps, but please let me in."

The event was not a rock concert, although news reporters compared it to one. It was the First International World Wide Web Conference, held in Geneva, Switzerland, in 1994.

Tim Berners-Lee, the man people were lining up to hear speak, is the inventor of the World Wide Web (WWW), also known simply as the Web. A global networked environment of interconnected documents and data accessible through the Internet, the WWW has lived up to its name. People across the planet have access to and contribute to the Web, which includes information on almost every topic imaginable.

The World Wide Web has come a long way since its quiet debut on Christmas Day 1990. Shortly after the 1994 convention, Tim's creation began to change dramatically the way many people in the world work, play, learn, and communicate. And it continues to expand its influence, as people add new Web pages every day. The Web has grown so fast that Tim has compared it to a bobsled. You have to push a bobsled to get it started. For a little way, it can be hard going. Then the bobsled starts going faster. Finally, it's whizzing downhill so rapidly there's no stopping it.

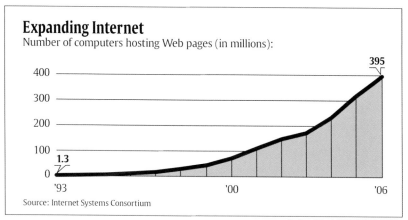

By Sam Ward, USA TODAY, 2008

In the twenty-first century, Tim's role is to safeguard the Web and to develop its potential. As important as Tim's invention has become, he believes he can make it even better. "The Web," says Berners-Lee, "is far from 'done.'"

Early computer: Conway Berners-Lee and Mary Lee Woods met while working on the Manchester University Mark 1 (*above*) in the late 1940s.

Fascinated by Computers

■■■■

"I happened to be in the right place at the right time," Timothy Berners-Lee has said about the invention of the Web, "and I happened to have the right combination of experience in my background." To many children growing up in the 1960s, computers sounded like a wonder from the far future, something akin to robots in science fiction movies. Tim knew better. Both his parents were mathematicians and computer pioneers.

Conway Berners-Lee and Mary Lee Woods met in the late 1940s, while they were working on the Manchester University Mark 1. Completed in 1949, the Mark 1 was one of the world's first computers. Tim's parents played pivotal roles in the development of the Mark 1, and his mother has even been called the world's first commercial computer programmer.

After they married, Conway and Mary Lee settled in London, England. Their son Timothy John was born on June 8, 1955. The oldest of four children, Tim grew up fascinated by his parents' work. He was a bright, curious little boy who liked to play in the park near his home and to go on picnics with his family in the countryside. Tim loved the fresh air and freedom of these outings. In contrast, London was an enormous, crowded place, but Tim felt happy in his special section of the city, called East Sheen.

About the time he started school, Tim's parents took him to visit their workplace. An early computer, which loomed taller than a refrigerator, delighted Tim. Wide-eyed, he surveyed the nearby desk where

IN FOCUS

Early Computers

The Manchester Mark 1 was developed out of a much smaller machine nicknamed the Baby, which was first run on June 21, 1948. Less than one year later, the Mark 1 was installed in the University of Manchester. Only scientists had access to the powerful computer.

But mathematicians such as Tim's parents envisioned a computer that would be available to more people. Building on the Mark 1, they helped develop the Ferranti Mark 1, which has been called "the world's first commercially available general purpose computer."

the computer programmer sat. It had a clock and a special contraption for paper tape. At that time, programmers punched holes into the rolls of tape to tell computers what to do.

Tim's parents didn't exactly say it in words, but their excitement over computers conveyed a message loud and clear to their son. Years later, he summed it up enthusiastically. "What you can do with computers is only limited by your imagination."

Back at his home, Tim put his imagination to good use. He attached two cardboard shoe boxes to the front of his toy chest and then went in search of paper tape. Because his parents were programmers, his house was full of it. Usually Tim liked to unravel the long roles of tape. This time he threaded the tape carefully through the shoe boxes. He had created his own play computer.

When their children were young, Mary Lee and Conway decided not to own a television. Instead of watching TV, Tim and siblings Peter, Helen, and Michael spent time making things. Tim liked to rummage through a drawer of odds and ends that he called the "scrap mat"

Paper tape: Early computers used paper tape to input information for calculation. The information would then transfer over a wire to a teleprinter, which would display or print the answer.

(scrap materials) box. Selecting his pieces carefully, Tim would glue together springs, bits of tubing, or perhaps the nozzle of a hose. He was proud of his unique creations.

Tim began elementary school at the age of five, but he learned to read from road signs rather than schoolbooks. On his way to play in the park, Tim passed street signs that were only 2 feet (0.6 meters) off the ground—the perfect height for a small boy. Tim liked to trace the clear black letters and smaller red letters with his finger. Before long, he was figuring out what street or district the letters stood for.

Tim didn't have to build all his playthings. He had a model train that ran on a fancy set of railroad tracks through tunnels and around sweeping arcs. But as he got older, his urge to tinker took over. Soon he was building electronic devices to make the train whistle or change directions. Then something unexpected happened. Tim discovered he liked electronics more than he liked the trains themselves.

Electronics went hand in hand with math, another of Tim's early interests. His parents enjoyed discussing math during meals. They could make simple lessons out of almost anything. "The whole point about mathematics in our house was that it was fun," Tim recalled. "We were always joking."

Young Experimenter

At school, Tim had two friends who liked science as much as he did. Tim spent his recess and other free time conducting science experiments with Nicholas Barton and Christopher Butler. The boys made electromagnets by wrapping wire around old iron nails. Eagerly they explored a variety of chemistry activities. They also built a cart with wheels from an old baby buggy and proudly rode it through the park.

 Tim and his pals had a handbook to help them explore science. *The Book of Experiments*, written by Leonard De Vries in the early 1900s, featured dozens of activities with such interesting titles as "Pick Up Teacups with a Balloon," "How to Make a Water Trombone," and "A Banana Skins Itself." Thanks to the World Wide Web, a new generation of aspiring scientists can access the book online.

Off to High School

When the boys turned eleven, it was time for them to change schools. Students in England attend high school at an earlier age than in the United States. Nicholas and Christopher went to the nearby grammar school (the equivalent of a U.S. high school). Tim's parents decided to send him to the prestigious Emanuel School. They felt Emanuel would provide a strong learning environment.

Situated in southwest London, Emanuel was an all-boys' school at that time. Tim appreciated the location, which was sandwiched between two railroad tracks. He liked to watch the trains coming and going much more than he enjoyed riding them.

Although he missed his grade-school friends, Tim had fun. He still loved the outdoors and enjoyed hiking with the new friends he made. Tramping the countryside during weekends or vacations, the boys sometimes stayed in youth hostels—small, affordable inns

High school: Tim attended Emanuel School in Battersea Rise, a section of southwest London.

designed especially for young people. After exploring England, they climbed hills in Wales and Scotland.

Hiking was far more satisfying to Tim than the athletic program at his school. Everyone was required to play rugby (a game similar to football) and cricket (something like baseball). Tim felt more comfortable doing calculations than catching balls. All he could do was hope that the ball would not come flying in his direction. When he got a little older, Tim chose rowing over sports that involved running and chasing balls. He didn't mind the hard work of plying the oars and enjoyed the water and the exercise.

 Tim's favorite books were mysteries and science fiction. Sometimes he became so engrossed in a good science fiction book that he stayed up all night reading. Even though he knew he would be tired the next day, he had to get to the end of the story.

At Emanuel, Tim's math teacher, Frank Grundy, especially inspired him. Mr. Grundy had a twinkle in his eye and a passion for math that his students appreciated. Although disorder often reigned in the classroom, Mr. Grundy understood his students well. He knew who needed help and who could use an extra challenge. The added work kept Tim from being bored. But even extra problems could not keep Tim busy all period. When students finished their assignments early, Mr. Grundy allowed them to play card games. Tim became a regular at the card table.

Chemistry teacher Derek "Daffy" Pennel also made a lasting impression on Tim. Mr. Pennel encouraged Tim to take chemistry his final

IN F⊕CUS

Just a Hunch

Many leading scientists, including Albert Einstein and Jonas Salk, have said that intuition was important in their work. Inventor Philo Farnsworth shared their approach to creativity. At the age of fourteen, he made an intuitive connection between the straight lines a plow makes in the earth and the lines of electrons forming on a screen. Philo's brilliant hunch led to the invention of electronic television.

Philo Farnsworth

year. Tim's schedule was already full, but he took the class anyway and still got A's in all his math and science classes.

Tim wanted to study computers too. Although computer science was a growing field, few schools offered classes in the subject at that time. One day Tim came upon his father working on a speech for his boss. Conway was mulling over books about the brain. Tim was curious. What did the brain have to do with computers? That was what Tim's father wanted to know too. One thing that makes the brain special is intuition, he explained.

Intuition is the way our brains make imaginative leaps from one topic to another. Perhaps it can be best described as creative hunches that go beyond logic. Computers did not make that kind of connection. But what if they could? Tim and his father talked it over on several occasions. They couldn't answer the question, but a computer that could make intuitive leaps would be powerful indeed. The idea lodged itself in Tim's mind.

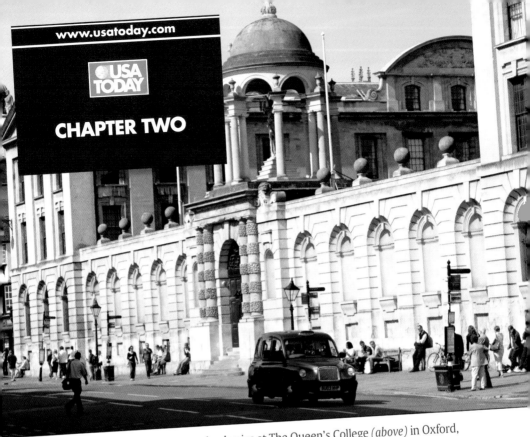

Off to college: Tim chose to study physics at The Queen's College (*above*) in Oxford, England, after he finished high school.

A Job That's Fun

■■■■

When the time came for Tim to attend college, he chose Oxford, one of the top universities in England. In 1973 eighteen-year-old Tim entered The Queen's College, which is part of Oxford. Perhaps intuition played some role in Tim's decision to major in physics, the study of energy and matter. Tim thought it would be theoretical like math and practical like electronics, two of his favorite subjects.

The Queen's College is one of forty-six colleges that make up the historic University of Oxford. The college was founded in 1341 by a chaplain to Queen Philippa.

Like all students at Oxford, Tim was assigned a tutor to follow his progress and to provide academic help and encouragement. John Moffatt helped Tim through the complexities of physics. Tim appreciated his patience and insight. When Tim made a mistake, John Moffatt didn't just guide him in the right direction. He showed that he appreciated Tim's originality. "This is intriguing the way you are doing things," he might say.

 One day at Oxford, Tim learned that some of his friends were taking a bus to nearby Cambridge University. Tim's childhood friend Nicholas attended Cambridge. Tim wanted to join his friends on the bus, but there was a hitch. Although tiddledywinks is usually considered a child's game, Oxford had a tiddledywinks team. You had to belong to the team to get a ride. Tim needed little coaxing to join. He visited Nicholas, played tiddledywinks, and had a great time.

College was an exciting time for Tim. He worked hard, made good friends, and went punting on the river. Pushing against the riverbed with a long pole, he steered his flat-bottomed boat through the shallow water. Tim also got involved in a campus event called Rag Week, which involved "lots of crazy events" as well as collections for charities. As a member of Rag Week's organizing committee, Tim decided to print one hundred copies of a list with all the volunteers' names. Personal computers and printers were not widely available yet. So Tim and his friend Pete Hammersly slipped stealthily into the systems area of the big physics computer. They were eager to do a secret printing job.

Rag Week is a traditional event at many colleges in England. The phrase may have originated during the 1800s when students gathered rags to give to the poor. The word *rag* can also mean "to bother or heckle someone." Students may have "ragged" passersby until they made a contribution to charity. To many people, rag has come to mean "raise and give."

The control room was deserted, and the printer was full of paper. All Tim and Pete had to do was to run upstairs to the computer itself and give the command to print the list. In record time, they completed the task and pounded downstairs to collect their copies. To their dismay, people were milling about frantically. Even worse, Joyce Clark, the systems manager, was reading their list as the copies slid out of the printer. The boys realized that one of the systems had gone down. They couldn't have picked a worse time for their stunt. "You! You!" cried Joyce, pointing at Tim and Peter. "Off!" And marching to the computer terminal, the angry manager deleted them as authorized users.

Tim's First Computer

No setback could stop Tim for long. If he couldn't use the university's computer, perhaps he could build one. He had already been planning to make his own monitor, or visual display unit (VDU). Tim began tinkering with a broken secondhand television set. Although it still couldn't receive broadcast transmissions, the television was good enough for Tim's purposes. Before long, he managed to produce vertical and horizontal lines on the screen. Next, he needed something like a keyboard.

During a school vacation, Tim worked at a sawmill. Part of his job was to climb a stack of wood and from there empty large trash cans of sawdust into a dumpster. One day as he was about to pour out the sawdust, he saw an old adding machine at the bottom of the dumpster. It probably didn't work anymore, but it had numerous buttons that Tim could use. He lugged his prize home and rearranged the letters so it looked like a keyboard. As a final touch, Tim bought a computer part called a character generator chip. The chip would make the letters appear on the VDU when he hooked it up to his computer.

Then Tim had a stroke of luck. About the time he graduated from Oxford in 1976, a new microprocessor was made available to the public. Microprocessors are small chips that direct the basic workings of a

Small but powerful: Intel 8080 microprocessor chips *(above)* were the first microprocessors powerful enough to run a computer and small enough to fit in a compact-sized computer, or a personal computer.

computer. Tim no longer had to connect his VDU to another computer. Instead, he used the microprocessor as the heart of his own computer. He simply built the other parts around the microprocessor. Tim connected his new computer to the VDU. The setup allowed him to store data and play games.

Young Computer Programmer

Tim graduated from Oxford in 1976 with a degree in physics. It was time to decide on a career. Tim was willing to work hard, but he wanted a job that was fun too. He thought of the fun he had had making his own computer. He thought of his parents who loved their work and talked about it enthusiastically. Computers excited Tim in a way that

IN FOCUS

One Invention Leads to Another

Dr. Ted Hoff Jr. is credited with developing the first microprocessor, the computer chip that made the computer revolution possible. A chip (also called a microchip) is a small, thin slice of a semiconductor material. Electricity is able to flow through a semiconductor but not as strongly as a full conductor would allow. Circuits in a chip route the electrical current and direct the way the computer works.

As an employee for Intel in 1969, Hoff was asked to work with some engineers from a Japanese company.

They had designed a small calculator with twelve semiconductor chips. Hoff felt he could redesign the calculator with a single chip. After the Japanese company approved Hoff's ideas, Intel engineers worked for nine months to create the first microprocessor. Labeled the 4004, it was a silicon-based chip only $\frac{1}{8}$ of an inch (0.3 centimeters) long and $\frac{1}{16}$ of an inch (0.2 cm) wide. But it was as powerful as the original ENIAC computer, built in 1946, which weighed 30 tons (27 metric tons).

IN F⊕CUS

A Tiny Powerhouse

Tim and his friends grew up in a great time for people who loved to tinker with electronics. "As we needed new devices, they became available," Tim explains. The electromagnets Tim made by wrapping wires around nails enabled him to build relay circuits. He could use these circuits to make burglar alarms. When Tim was in high school, transistors became available. Transistors made it possible to control electrical current and make his electronic gadgets work even better. In college, Tim made use of another new development—logic chips. Logic chips packed many transistors into a very tiny space. When Tim was putting his visual display unit together, he could use logic chips to help him achieve horizontal and vertical lines. The advent of microprocessors, as Tim was about to graduate from college, made it easy for him to turn his VDU into a true computer. The microprocessor gave him a huge advantage. But Tim could have built a very primitive computer out of electromagnets if he had to. "By then I understood how computers worked from top to bottom," he says.

nothing else did. His next step seemed clear. He began interviewing for jobs in the computer industry.

Tim took a job as a software engineer at Plessey Telecommunications in the city of Poole in a part of England called Dorset. The setting on the coast of the English Channel enchanted him as much as the job itself. When Tim arrived for his interview, he could smell the ocean and watch seagulls circling above the town.

Two years later, Tim received a call from his friend Kevin Rogers. Kevin worked for a small company in Ferndown, England, that was pioneering software for printers. "Tim, there's work here for two," Kevin declared. "I think they should hire you too." Soon the company's owners, Dennis Nash and John Poole, did just that. Thanks to microprocessors, computers were becoming smaller, more powerful, and less expensive. Tim was at the head of an exciting new phase in the development of personal computers. "[Riding] the crest of the wave" is the way he later remembered it. Tim "rode the wave" in another way too. He had great times windsurfing with Kevin.

CERN

In mid-1979, Tim left his job to become an independent consultant. Computers were becoming more widely used in business. Companies hired Tim to design microprocessor systems. This new position gave Tim the chance to travel. He was on a job in Zug, Switzerland, when Kevin Rogers told him about another opportunity. Soon the two friends were on a train speeding through mountainous terrain toward a very special destination—CERN, in the Swiss city of Geneva.

CERN, the world's largest particle physics laboratory, straddles the Swiss-French border between the Alps and the Jura Mountains. CERN is one of the top centers for physics research in the world. It requires powerful computer systems to keep track of the data from the many experiments conducted there.

New sights: CERN lies just outside Geneva, Switzerland (*above*), and near the Swiss border with France.

Smaller and smaller: As scientists developed new technology in the 1970s and 1980s, computers got smaller and smaller. The NCR Tower 1632 *(top left)* was a typical computer in 1975. The Apple II *(top right)* came with its own carrying case. The IBM Model AT personal computer *(bottom left)* dominated the market in the mid-1980s. Compaq introduced the laptop *(bottom right)* in the late 1980s.

High Energy

Scientists come to CERN from all over the world to study the tiny particles that make up all physical matter. Because these particles are smaller than the smallest atoms, they are called subatomic. Many experiments at CERN involve sending subatomic particles through long tunnels at supersonic speeds. The tunnels are called particle accelerators. As the particles speed through the tunnels, they often bump into one another. The collisions make interesting things happen. Sometimes entirely new particles are formed. Studying the new particles, scientists try to understand the secrets of the universe. In 2008 CERN tested the Large Hadron Collider (LHC), the world's highest energy particle accelerator.

Flying particles: This model of the LHC gives visitors to CERN a good idea of what the particle accelerator looks like.

During their interviews for positions at CERN, Tim and Kevin visited the control room. The rows of glowing dials and electronic equipment filled Tim with a sense of adventure. He thought the room was "an electronic engineer's paradise." He accepted a six-month position and settled happily into the hillside cabin where he was assigned to work.

One of Tim's responsibilities was to keep track of the different computers and software programs that the scientists used. The problem was that Tim didn't have a very good memory for names or for that kind of detail. What Tim needed was a computer system to help him to organize all the facts.

Tim had a quick, sharp mind. When he wanted a piece of information, he wanted it fast. If he had to remember what experiments one scientist was doing, he wanted to be able to type in the name and find exactly what he needed. He disliked the in-between steps, during which the computer narrowed its search. Tim thought there had to be an easier, better way to organize material on a computer.

www.usatoday.com

CHAPTER THREE

Web design: Tim thought information should be stored so it would be interconnected.

Enquire Within

Twenty-five-year-old Tim worked rapidly when it came to writing computer programs for physics experiments. His energy and enthusiasm impressed his coworkers. According to one colleague, Tim could complete his assigned tasks in about half an hour. That left him the rest of the day to develop his own ideas. And Tim had plenty of ideas! "Sometimes [they were] completely wacky," remembers one coworker, "and sometimes quite brilliant."

A Spider's Web

One of Tim's ideas was so powerful that he couldn't stop thinking about it. It had to do with the way that documents were stored in CERN's computers. And it just might hold the answer to remembering people's names, experiments, and computer programs. Instead of linking documents in an electronic hierarchy like a ladder, what if they were connected randomly?

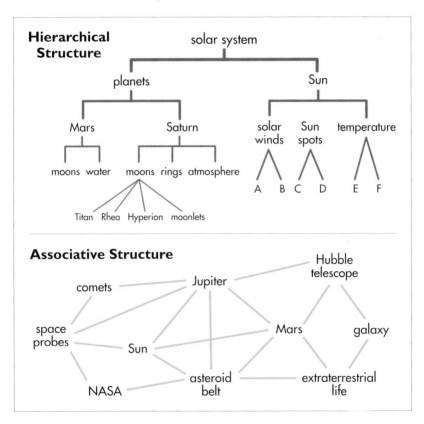

Structure: In a hierarchical structure, connections between topics have a clear order from highest to lowest. Everything is neatly placed in a category. There are no horizontal connections between categories. You cannot jump from the moonlets of Saturn directly to the solar winds. The organization is from top to bottom. In an associative structure, individual topics can be linked in many ways. It is easy to move from topic to topic through links.

Soon Tim was working on a new computer program to test his idea and to help him keep track of everything happening at CERN. He jokingly called it his "play program" because it was so much fun to develop. He officially named it Enquire, after an old reference book his parents owned called *Enquire Within Upon Everything*. Tim had rarely opened the book while growing up, but he liked the title. The words had a sort of magic ring to them, an "open sesame" to pathways of knowledge.

The program Tim had in mind would allow him to establish pathways too. It would help him to find his way through the maze of people, programs, and experiments at CERN.

Creating Enquire

Tim began to create Enquire with a single page, called a node. To establish another page, he had to create a link to the original node. Every new node had to be logically linked to a previous node. Establishing the links was relatively simple. And accessing the information afterward was easy too. The Enquire program stored relationships among people, programs, and ideas in a way that was different from any other computer program. Connections, not hierarchies, were the key feature of Tim's concept. Tim hoped that a person might even stumble upon "information which he did not realize he needed to know." This was another bonus that other data-storing systems couldn't offer.

Enquire enabled Tim to keep track of all the names and research interests he needed to remember. He could jump easily from a scientist's name to that person's most recent experiment to a list of publications. The system worked so well that Tim thought other people at CERN would find it useful too. But Enquire would only work on the type of computer Tim used at CERN. Later, Tim created software so other types of computers could use Enquire, but information still could not be transferred easily between computers. The Internet, whose beginning can be traced to 1969, was still in its early stages. At this time, CERN's computers did not have access to the type of global communication the Internet could provide, although they did have access to some local networks.

Tim's imagination leaped ahead to a time when ideas could be exchanged between computers quickly and easily. "Suppose all the information stored on computers everywhere were linked." Tim pondered. "Suppose I could program my computer to create a space in which anything could be linked to anything." The possibilities were staggering.

IN FOCUS

Web Pioneers

Tim had no inkling that other individuals had considered ideas about linking electronic data that were similar to his own. As early as 1945, U.S. engineer Vannevar Bush published an article in the *Atlantic Monthly* magazine about a machine he called the Memex. The Memex stored documents and microfilm. More than that, it connected the original text with other documents to which it made reference. This was still a long way from what Tim wanted, but it did point in the same direction.

Twenty years later, in the 1960s, another computer pioneer came closer to what Tim had in mind. Ted Nelson developed what he called hypertext. *Hyper* means "above" or "beyond." Nelson's method of organization allowed readers to go above

or beyond the text immediately in front of them.

Normally a person reads a page in sequential order. Hypertext gives readers choices about where to go next. Suppose someone is reading about the solar system. Halfway down the page, she sees the word *Mars* in highlighted text. The highlighting shows there is an available link between what she is reading and another document that gives more detailed information about Mars. The reader can follow that link and then return to the original text or go to another link leading off the Mars document.

Ted Nelson hoped that one day all human knowledge would be linked together through hypertext. He named his ambitious project Xanadu, referring to a mythical place of luxury.

Back to England

Tim didn't have a chance to expand Enquire. Just as his six-month consulting job at CERN was ending, he got a phone call from his former boss John Poole. John had started a new company, Image Computer Systems Limited, and he needed someone to help develop software. Would Tim be interested?

Both Tim and Kevin Rogers said yes to John's offer. Before he left CERN, Tim gave the computer disk with the Enquire program to one of the systems managers. He explained that Enquire had helped him to keep track of people and experiments at CERN. Maybe someone else could use it too, he suggested. Tim returned to England, leaving all copies of the program behind.

 After Tim became famous, his former boss John Poole talked about him in England's *Guardian* newspaper. Poole described Tim as "amenable and easy to talk to; he is very clever; and he is very dogged. Those things together are what has made him a success."

High praise: Some of Tim's coworkers described him using the same three words—intense, efficient, and creative.

Enter the Internet

Tim was happy to be back in England. He enjoyed his work developing software for printers that produced fancy graphics. The company did well, and John Poole credited Tim with much of its prosperity. But after about three years, Tim felt the urge to live abroad again. It was time for new adventures and new challenges. Tim recalled his experience in Switzerland—his keen enjoyment of the people, the place, and his job. Soon he knew exactly what he wanted to do.

In the spring of 1983, Tim applied for a job at CERN. His boss wrote a recommendation for Tim, praising him as "an intense, efficient and creative worker." Several other colleagues wrote references too. Later, they were surprised that they had used the same three words to describe Tim!

When the time came for Tim to return to Switzerland in September 1984, John gave him a very special gift—his own Compaq computer. Most computers in the mid-1980s were very large and intended for

May 21, 2007

25 years of 'eureka' moments

From the Pages of USA TODAY

We're a nation of inventors in garages and corporate labs, creating gadgets and services that delight us and occasionally drive us crazy. On its 25th anniversary USA TODAY chose 25 inventions that changed our lives in the years since 1982:

TOP 25 Life-changing inventions

1 Cellphones

Car phones were around in the 1970s, but it wasn't until 1983 that Motorola introduced the first widely available handheld cellphone. The DynaTAC 8000x weighed almost 2 pounds, but it still cost $3,995.

2 Laptop computers

It was about as portable as a sewing machine. But the 28-pound Compaq Portable Compaq Computer's very first product was the first portable IBM-compatible PC on the market. More than 53,000 sold in the year after its 1983 launch, despite a price usually topping $3,000.

government agencies or large organizations. A few computer businesses, however, including the Compaq Computer Corporation, had
designed much smaller computers for individuals. The Compaq computer was advertised as "one of the first portable computers." Years
later, Tim recalled that its bulkiness reminded him of a sewing machine.
Compared to modern computers, it was heavy and cumbersome. But
at the time, Tim was delighted with his gift. He had a computer he
could take wherever he went, even if awkwardly.

[Other items on the list are as follows:]
  3 BlackBerries
  4 Debit cards
  5 Caller ID
  6 DVDs
  7 Lithium rechargeable batteries
  8 iPods
  9 Pay at the [gas] pump
 10 Lettuce in a bag
 11 Digital cameras
 12 Doppler radar
 13 Flat-panel TVs
 14 Electronic tolls
 15 PowerPoint
 16 Microwavable popcorn
 17 High-tech footwear
 18 Online stock trading
 19 Big Bertha gold clubs
 20 Disposable contacts
 21 StairMaster
 22 TiVo
 23 Purell
 24 Home satellite TV
 25 Karaoke

—Researched and written by USA TODAY's Byron Acohido, Jim Hopkins,
Jefferson Graham and Michelle Kessler, May 21, 2007

Back at CERN

When Tim arrived at CERN, the scientists were excited about the new particle accelerator that was being built. Tim was assigned to a team directed by Peggie Rimmer that was working on a special computer system. It was called FASTBUS, and it was designed to help other computer systems gather information about atomic particles.

The new accelerator under construction at CERN in the 1980s would be much bigger than any of its predecessors. Called the Large Electron-Positron Collider (LEP), the round tunnel was almost 17 miles (27 kilometers) in circumference. It began almost 330 feet (100 meters) beneath CERN and went for almost 1,000 feet (300 meters) to the foothills of the Jura Mountains along the border of Switzerland and France. CERN completed the accelerator in 1989 and used it through 2000. At that point, it was dismantled to make room for the construction of the Large Hadron Collider (LHC), which was first tested in 2008.

Warming to the challenge, Tim began thinking up new ways to improve FASTBUS. Some mornings the computer group would find that a program had been upgraded or changed in some way. Tim had been working after hours again! Why hadn't he told them about his plans beforehand his coworkers wanted to know. Tim protested that the changes were so good he just had to make them at once.

Tim speaks softly but rapidly—sometimes too rapidly. When Tim explained his ideas at CERN meetings, his words came so quickly that colleagues had trouble understanding him. Sometimes they asked him to speak in French to slow him down.

Sharing Data

Because he worked so rapidly, Tim had plenty of free time to think about the ways in which computers stored information. Another computer system called CERNDOC had recently been put into effect. Like other computer systems, CERNDOC stored data and documents in a hierarchical structure

But was this really the best way to handle huge amounts of information? Tim believed that his old Enquire program was better for storing experiments and ideas than CERNDOC was. On first returning to Switzerland, Tim had been disappointed to learn that his original Enquire disk had been misplaced. But he quickly re-created the program on his own Compaq and on the computer he was assigned to use at CERN. The second version of Enquire wasn't as good as his original program, but it furthered Tim's vision of what Enquire could be.

Enquire still worked only on individual computers. Tim wanted as many computers as possible to be able to communicate easily with one another. Part of his work for CERN involved writing special codes that allowed one computer to direct the workings of another computer. This code is called Remote Procedure Call, or RPC. Tim found this work fascinating. But RPC had limits. It did not allow scientists to share data and documents across their varied computer systems.

Then Tim discovered another technology that promised to do even more than RPC. He began exploring the Internet. Although the history of the Internet dates back to the 1960s, the general public still knew little about it in the 1980s. Unless you were a computer expert, trying to use the Internet was a complicated matter. E-mail existed, but few people outside of universities had access to it. But Tim felt the Internet had vast potential to help people share information.

 Many people confuse the Internet with the World Wide Web, but the two are not the same. Tim has called the Internet "a network of networks." These complicated connections allow computers to communicate with one another. The World Wide Web gives people around the globe the technologies needed to share a wealth of information via the Internet. The Internet existed before the World Wide Web. But the World Wide Web, as we know it, could not exist without the Internet.

"A Miniature for the Rest of the World"

Gradually an idea took shape in Tim's mind. What if he combined hypertext with the Internet? Hypertext would allow computer users to follow links from highlighted phrases to other documents. With the Internet, it wouldn't matter where the other documents were located. A researcher would be able to access information down the hall or from a colleague's computer in a foreign country.

Tim's plan was different from other systems in another important way. No one computer would control everything. Transfer of information would take place directly between computers. There would be no central station through which all documents had to be routed. Pages of documents could be stored on any number of computers. People could go from document to document easily, regardless of where they were stored.

It's impossible to know exactly how many computers have access to the Internet or are on the Internet at any given time. The Internet was set up originally to hold 4.2 billion Internet Protocol (IP) addresses. An IP address is the numeric version of the Web address computer users type into a browser's address bar. IP addresses enable computers and other devices to connect to the Internet. By 2008 nearly all the 4.2 billion IP addresses had been taken but not just by computers. Web servers, cable modems, routers, and other devices also require IP addresses. Internet planners were prepared for the shortage with Internet Protocol Version 6 (IPv6). This system allows for up to 340,282,366,920,938,463,463,374,607,431,768,211,456 (340 undecillion) Internet addresses!

Tim could scarcely contain his excitement. He knew he could develop a system that would make it easy for everyone to find and share information. But he needed time and support. Would CERN allow him to take time from his other work? Would it give him what he needed? There was only one way to find out. In March 1989, Tim submitted a proposal to his boss, Mike Sendall. In the proposal, Tim described what he wanted to do and why he thought it was important. He asked for the time and resources he needed to create his system.

Scientists at CERN would benefit greatly from Tim's proposed system. But Tim was already looking way beyond the physics community. In his proposal, he called the computer system at CERN "a model in miniature for the rest of the world in a few years' time." He believed that his network of information would someday spread across the globe and change life for everyone.

IN FOCUS

The Origin of the Internet

The Internet indirectly owes its beginning to the advent of the Space Age (1957 to 1986), an era of rapid development of space technology. In 1957 the Soviet Union launched *Sputnik*, the world's first artificial satellite. At that time, the United States and the Soviet Union were in tense political, military, and technological competition. Alarmed that the Soviet Union had gotten into outer space before the United States, President Dwight D. Eisenhower established the Advanced Research Projects Agency (ARPA). The purpose of the agency was to overcome the Soviet lead in science and technology.

In 1962 J. C. R. Licklider, a computer scientist at ARPA, envisioned a global network of interconnected computers. Although he left ARPA before he could start the ambitious project, others became interested in his concept. Bob Taylor and Larry Roberts were two of the top men involved in planning the ARPA computer network, or ARPANET. According to one prevalent view, the goal of the project was to provide a communication system that could survive a nuclear attack. In reality, Licklider simply wanted to help scientists exchange information more easily.

Telephone lines could be used to establish links between the computers. But how could scientists send the information stored in each computer along the lines? Scientist Leonard Kleinrock tackled that problem. Relying on the work of American Paul Baran and Englishman Donald Davies, he developed a system of "packet switching." Kleinrock made it possible to divide information into small packets that could be transferred easily between computers.

Leonard Kleinrock

Paul Baran

with one another because they did not follow the same rules for sending information. What was needed was a standard that all computer networks would use. A man named Vint Cerf addressed the problem in 1974. He wrote a new set of rules for sending information between computers. It was called Transmission Control Protocol, or TCP. After TCP became the accepted standard, the different computer networks could be joined leading to a true Internet, or "network of networks." For his valuable contribution, Vint Cerf is sometimes called the father of the Internet.

The ARPANET officially began in 1969 when computers at four U.S. colleges were linked—the University of California at Los Angeles, Stanford University, the University of California at Santa Barbara, and the University of Utah. Each main computer connected to a specially designed "gateway" computer. These smaller computers were called Interface Message Processors, or IMPs. At the sending end, an IMP divided the message into packets. At the receiving end, an IMP reassembled the message and sent it on to the main computer.

As the ARPANET expanded, other computer networks were also coming into existence. But the various networks could not communicate

Vint Cerf

At work: Tim's proposal was outside the bounds of the usual work at CERN. He continued to work on the projects CERN assigned to him while waiting for his proposal to be approved.

WWW

■ ■ ■ ■

Tim's boss at CERN sensed the importance of Tim's proposal, even though he found it confusing. "I could not figure out what it was, but I thought it was great," recalled Mike Sendall.[1] Eager to know what Tim would do next, Sendall wrote, "And now?" on the last page of the proposal.

But other people had to look at the proposal before it could be approved. No one at CERN really had the authority to give Tim the money, time, and equipment he needed. The project was not directly related to physics. It was outside the scope of CERN's mission. Tim waited and waited for a definite response.

Hoping to generate more interest for his project, Tim discussed his ideas with his colleagues at CERN. Some were enthusiastic, but many of them expressed little interest. Most of his coworkers were more concerned with physics than with a new information system. Although Tim understood this attitude, he was disappointed by it.

Meanwhile, Tim studied everything available about hypertext. He also continued to use the Internet. The more he learned, the more Tim was convinced he was on to something important. But months passed without an official response to his proposal.

Other Engagements

Still waiting for a reply to his proposal at CERN, Tim attended a performance of the play *Goodbye Charlie* one evening. An attractive young actress in the lead role caught his attention. Sometime later, he had

IN FOCUS

The Singing Computer Scientist

As absorbed as he was by computers, Tim had time and energy for other activities. One of his colleagues discovered that Tim liked to sing. An English singing group called the Geneva Amateur Operatic Society gave performances nearby. "I got roped into the cast of [the musical] *Oklahoma!*" Tim later recalled. He enjoyed the experience so much that he stuck around for many other roles. One of his favorite performances was *Peter Pan*, in which he played the nanny of the Darling children. In the British pantomime tradition, a man dressed as a woman plays the role of the nanny. Tim liked to make people laugh. He thought it was great fun to swing from cables as he "flew" across the stage to Neverland.

a chance to meet her. Nancy Carlson was a U.S. computer programmer and analyst working for the World Health Organization. Soon Tim and Nancy were spending a great deal of time together. They became engaged in 1989, and the young couple spent Christmas vacation with Nancy's parents in Fairfield, Connecticut. Tim enjoyed meeting his future in-laws and exploring New England.

Tim also took advantage of his time in the United States to pursue his passion for computers and hypertext. He visited Fermilab—a physics research lab near Chicago, Illinois—and learned all about their computer systems. Then he attended a workshop on hypertext in Maryland. If there had been any doubt in Tim's mind before the workshop, there was absolutely none afterward. CERN needed hypertext! More than ever, Tim was determined to supply that need.

 Fermilab is named after Nobel Prize-winning Italian physicist Enrico Fermi, who invented the first nuclear reactor in 1942. The lab is a U.S. counterpart to CERN. Scientists at Fermilab perform experiments with high-energy particle accelerators.

Exciting New Computer

Back at CERN, Tim learned that some researchers had received a new and powerful kind of computer named NeXT. Immediately, Tim realized that a NeXT computer was just the kind of machine he needed to bring hypertext and the Internet together. He took his mentor Ben Segal with him to talk to his boss Mike Sendall. Ben was an early enthusiast for the Internet and spent a lot of time trying to persuade CERN to use it. Tim thought he might need Ben's moral support in asking for a NeXT. After all, Tim's proposal still had not been officially approved. He couldn't just say he needed the NeXT to create his new information system.

Tim needn't have worried. "Let's get two NeXT computers," Mike said at once. And that wasn't all. "Why don't you see what it's like for developing a program?" Mike continued. "How about that hypertext program you talked about?" Tim noted the sparkle in his eye. It was almost as if Mike could read his mind.

IN F⊙CUS

As Fun as a Sports Car

The NeXT was the brainchild of computer designer Steve Jobs. NeXT was designed to be "a supercomputer in a small package." Sometimes it was called a "black box" because of its simple, elegant appearance. Its innovative technology and powerful drive aroused a great deal of interest among computer users. It even came with software that included access to all of Shakespeare's plays.

Tim once compared his NeXT to "a favorite sports car." Despite its many features, however, the NeXT was not commercially successful. Twice as expensive as other computers, it had limited software. Jobs tried and failed to get larger computer development companies interested in his machine.

Inventor's tool: Tim used this NeXT computer when he started the World Wide Web.

Marriage

While Tim was waiting for his NeXT computers to arrive, he redated his original proposal and redistributed it. Maybe this time he would get the support from CERN that he desperately needed. But Tim had something even more exciting on his mind than hypertext and the Internet. In 1990 Tim and Nancy were married at the Congregational Church in Fairfield, Connecticut.

When Tim and Nancy returned to Europe, they settled into a house in Switzerland. Later, they moved to a modest house in France near the Swiss border. Although their new home was small, it had a spectacular view. From their front yard, the young couple gazed across the city of Geneva to snow-covered Mont Blanc, the highest mountain in the Alps. The backyard presented a peaceful scene of green fields and grazing cows with the majestic Jura Mountains looming behind.

Surrounded by beauty, Tim continued to dream of his new information system and to wait for some official word from CERN. His second proposal hadn't aroused any more interest than his first. But Tim's determination to fulfill his vision only grew stronger.

A Surprising Collaboration

Tim finally found a person at CERN who was as excited about the hypertext project as he was. Robert Cailliau was a Belgian engineer and computer scientist whom Tim had known briefly at CERN in 1980. CERN is a huge complex and employs a lot of people. The two men might never have crossed paths again if it weren't for Mike Sendall. Talking to Robert one day, Mike realized that some of his ideas sounded very much like Tim's. "There's someone you should talk to," he said.

Robert went to visit Tim at his office, and the two found common ground at once. But in temperament and style, they could not have been more different. Robert was a stickler for details, while Tim preferred to focus more on the larger picture. Robert liked to make plans and to schedule things carefully, while Tim plowed through tasks on inspiration alone. Even the way they dressed marked them as opposites.

Belgian collaborator: Robert Cailliau worked with Tim to make Tim's hypertext project a reality.

Robert was very particular about his clothing. Tim paid less attention to what he wore. Despite their differences, however, their partnership worked. Pooling their talents, Tim and Robert were fast and effective workers.

As Tim continued to consider his new information system, Robert took another look at the proposal Tim had already written. He saw that it required a great deal of work. Although the basic ideas were all there, it needed more detail.

Tim and Robert set to work rewriting Tim's proposal. When they submitted the third version to CERN, the title read, "World Wide Web: Proposal for a Hypertext Project." It included all the important details that Tim didn't like to think about, such as staff requirements and cost and a schedule. Although this proposal got more attention, CERN still didn't give a full go-ahead.

A Catchy Name

Tim wanted a catchy name for his hypertext project. "Information Management" wasn't right. He wanted something more descriptive—a name that would be easy to abbreviate and to remember. Carefully, he considered his options. Information Mesh was one possibility. Since mesh can refer to a net or network, it seemed like a good description of what Tim wanted to do. But Tim thought that "mesh" sounded too much like the word *mess*. He didn't want people to think of his information system that way.

What about The Information Mine? Tim wondered. Just as treasure can be dug from a mine, knowledge could be gained from The Information Mine. It was a nice image, but almost immediately Tim saw a problem. He knew the phrase would be shortened to its initials, or the first letter of each word, which spelled TIM! An unassuming fellow, Tim did not want his information system named after himself.

Another idea occurred to Tim. He tried it out on his friends. "World Wide Web," he told them. His colleagues objected. World Wide Web would almost certainly be reduced to its initials, they pointed out. WWW was quite a mouthful of syllables. It wasn't simple and snappy enough. But Tim loved the name. He knew it was perfect for what he had in mind. As more people began putting information on the Web, users in the United States or Europe would be able to access data stored in computers in Africa, South America, and even Antarctica. His system would be truly global.

The Hypertext Community

Despite this frustration, the fall of 1990 was an exciting time for Tim. His NeXT computers finally arrived, and he went to Versailles, France, for a conference on hypertext. Different businesses displayed software that allowed people to use hypertext. As he strolled through the exhibits, two companies especially intrigued Tim. Their hypertext software reminded him of the way he wanted to present material on the

Web. Tim explained to the software representatives that if the Internet were connected to their software, a whole new way of sharing information would be born. Instead of following links to other documents stored only on their own computers, users would be able to follow links to documents stored all over the world.

But the company representatives did not understand what Tim was trying to tell them. A web of information that spanned the globe seemed highly impractical. Hypertext had not been very successful financially. Perhaps Tim's vision just sounded too good to be true.

A Window of Time

Disappointed once again, Tim realized that few other people were interested in his system. Tim had his NeXT computer. He had Robert to help with organization and with practical matters such as finding workspace and generating interest among their colleagues. Most of all, Tim had an enthusiasm that bubbled up inside him and refused to let him rest. He was supposed to be working on computer programs to control particle accelerators. But at the time, CERN staff was in between experiments. The LEP accelerator, so important when Tim arrived at CERN, was shut down, and scientists were awaiting the opening of a new accelerator. This time gap was just what Tim needed, and Mike Sendall was behind Tim all the way. Mike pretended not to know what was happening as Tim sat down and began working out the code for the World Wide Web.

Pieces of history: Tim's NeXT computer and the original proposal for the World Wide Web are on display at the CERN museum.

Up and Running

Creating the World Wide Web was exhilarating for Tim. The job itself was fairly straightforward, but he believed that the end result would revolutionize the way people used computers. Tim worked intensely and quickly. After a full day at CERN, he drove home, often stopping at a supermarket to pick up something for dinner. Sometimes he and Nancy went out to dinner at one of the many nice restaurants nearby.

Day after day, Tim worked energetically. When he needed a break, he headed to Tortella's

Café, a restaurant near CERN that was a popular meeting spot for scientists from CERN. He always found lots of people there willing to listen to Tim's progress reports. Tim gestured dramatically and spoke rapidly when he was excited about something. His colleagues could not help but be intrigued.

The program Tim was developing would allow users to create hypertext pages. Certain words or phrases would be highlighted, inviting people to follow them to new documents, or Web pages. The user could follow links indefinitely through a world of information.

Locating a Web Page

How would the computer know where to find the Web page the user wanted? Tim had a solution for that. Each Web page would have its own Universal Document Identifier (UDI). Later, they became known as Uniform Resource Locators, or URLs. Basically, a URL is an address that tells the computer where to find the Web page the user has requested. A computer with software that stores the information code for a large number of websites is called a Web server. Most Web servers are high-memory computers located in companies, universities, or government offices.

Not every computer connecting to the Web is a Web server. A computer that provides its users with access to the World Wide Web and translates the information code—but doesn't store Web pages—is called a Web client. The computers people use at home or at school are usually Web clients. Most likely, they do not contain Web pages that can be accessed from other computers. But Web clients do have software that allows a user to see what sorts of pages are available on the World Wide Web. Tim referred to this type of software as a browser. Computer users type a URL into their browser's address bar to get to a particular website.

Communication between Computers

Tim was making progress. But what if a Web client wanted information that was stored in a Web server that used a different computer

IN FOCUS

Decoding a Web Address

Web addresses can look complicated, but they're not hard to understand when you break them down. Consider the following website:

http://www.w3.org/People/Berners-Lee/Kids.html

http specifies the protocol, or set of rules for exchanging information between computers.

www tells you that the document is part of the World Wide Web.

w3.org indicates the server where the website is to be found. In this case, it is the server for the World Wide Web Consortium. Slashes following w3.org indicate folders, or different areas on the server. A folder on people includes a folder on Tim Berners-Lee, which includes his Web page for kids.

The last letters refer to the computer language used to code the Web documents. In this case, the text is coded in html.

---

language? It would be like a person who speaks only English asking directions from a person who speaks only Japanese.

Tim had an answer to this problem too. Tim wrote a new computer language called Hypertext Markup Language (HTML). A common language would make it possible to share information across computers. HTML has become the standard language of most hypertext documents on the Web.

The process Tim envisioned was simple. A Web client requests a particular URL from the Web server. In making the request, the Web client uses a special set of rules. These rules are called Hypertext Transfer Protocol, or HTTP. The Web server also uses HTTP to transfer the requested HTML document back to the Web client. It doesn't matter if the Web client and the Web server are a room away or half a world away from each other. HTTP, running on top of the Internet, guarantees that the full document can be transported to any computer anywhere.

Client and Server Communicating through HTTP

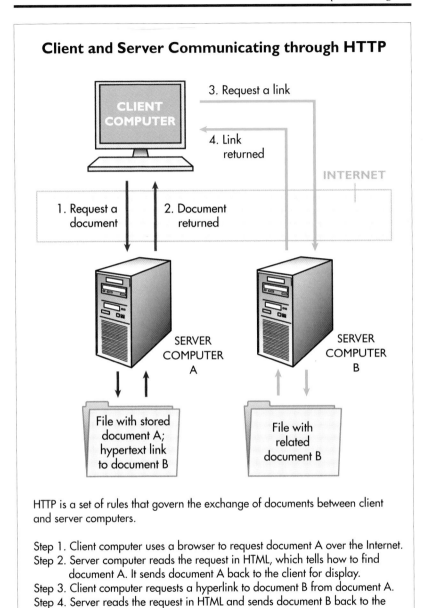

HTTP is a set of rules that govern the exchange of documents between client and server computers.

Step 1. Client computer uses a browser to request document A over the Internet.
Step 2. Server computer reads the request in HTML, which tells how to find document A. It sends document A back to the client for display.
Step 3. Client computer requests a hyperlink to document B from document A.
Step 4. Server reads the request in HTML and sends document B back to the client for display.

How it works: This diagram shows how Hypertext Transfer Protocol, the Internet, and a Web server work together to create the World Wide Web.

Using the Internet: These high school students in Atlanta, Georgia, are writing letters to students in Moscow, Russia, in 1991. They sent the letters via a modem linkup. The Internet was available before Tim's invention, but the Web revolutionized the way people used the Internet.

"An Enormous, Unbounded World"

When the information arrives at the Web client computer, it is formatted in HTML. Then the browser translates it from HTML into the patterns, headings, and text that make up the Web page. The Web page—text and graphics—appears on the computer screen. The document contains other hypertext phrases that link to other Web pages that link to others and others and so on. The process becomes an endless adventure. As Tim himself later wrote, "A single hypertext link could lead to an enormous, unbounded world."

For the Web to become that exciting, it would have to contain lots of thought-provoking and lively material. Tim could get the Web started. He could create a Web server and set all the mechanisms in place for the Web to grow. But once he had achieved this crucial beginning, it would be up to others to create links that would slowly expand the Web's reach.

Making rapid progress, Tim worked out the computer codes necessary to put the Web together. Within several months of beginning the project, Tim installed the first Web server and the first Web client onto his own NeXT. It was a small beginning. The entire system was contained within a single computer, but it was poised for growth. Tim gave World Wide Web read-write browser software to all the CERN scientists with NeXT computers. At last the Web was up and running. Christmas was only a few days off. In a spirit of festivity, Tim put the date December 25, 1990, on his programming documents.

 Many people have asked Tim how he got the idea for the World Wide Web. "When ideas form in your mind, you can't tell where they come from," he replies. "Half-formed ideas come into fuller ideas. Creativity happens. You can't look back and see how it happened."

Fatherhood

Despite a strong sense of achievement, Tim remained surprisingly calm. He was anticipating an even greater event. On New Year's Eve, Tim drove Nancy to the hospital through a raging snowstorm. The next day, their daughter, Alice, was born. Tim loved being a father. "As amazing as it would be to see the Web develop," he wrote years later, "it would never compare to seeing the development of our child."

An Exciting Phone Book

As he thought about the Web, Tim faced some big questions. What should he do with it next? Although Tim believed the Web would be extremely useful to people from all walks of life, he had created it at CERN. Did that mean he should refine the software to fit the needs of physicists looking for new subatomic particles? After all, CERN did pay his salary. Tim didn't really want the Web to be just for physicists, but he knew it had to be firmly established at CERN in order to spread elsewhere. This presented another problem. Although many scientists at CERN found the World Wide Web interesting, most weren't convinced that they needed it.

Tim and Robert came up with a plan to generate more enthusiasm. Scientists were continually coming and going at CERN. Other researchers from all over the world were also associated with the lab. This meant that phone numbers were constantly being added and deleted. If the CERN phone book were available on the World Wide Web, it would be easy to update phone numbers. Workers at CERN would always have access to the most recent information.

Connecting people: The campus of CERN covers more than 1,240 acres (500 hectares) and houses more than two thousand people. Tim's proposal would connect these researchers.

A great deal of work had to be done first. Someone would have to develop a Web server for CERN's big central computer, which stored the phone numbers. A man named Bernd Pollermann, who maintained CERN's central computer, agreed to complete this project. The server would let the big computer supply Web pages. The second requirement was supplying scientists with browsers for their own computers. Tim took on this job and also taught Bernd how to write HTML. The phone numbers would have to be formatted into HTML to become available on the Web.

Within several months, everything was in place. Tim visited researchers all over CERN to demonstrate the system. He showed everyone how to access the World Wide Web and how to look up phone numbers. People listened with interest. Getting the numbers they needed had never been so easy. The new phone book was a hit.

WHERE THE
WEB
WAS BORN

The beginning: Robert Cailliau stands next to a plaque commemorating the birth of the World Wide Web at CERN.

A Grassroots Effort

■■ ■■

Tim, Robert, Bernd, and Nicola Pellow (a student interning at CERN) worked hard to improve the Web and to increase its popularity at CERN. Sometimes small groups of researchers invited Tim to their offices so he could show them what the Web could do. Tim jumped at these opportunities. Despite the popularity of the phone book, he knew that the Web was still a hard sell. Many people were convinced that getting information from the Web would take too long to be practical.

Tim had realized all along that speed would be an important factor. When he pulled up documents in a fraction of a second, people were impressed. Yet even while they acknowledged the Web's speed, some scientists still weren't convinced of its usefulness. "Inventing the Web was actually rather straightforward," Tim commented much later. "Explaining to people that it was a good idea—helping them get over all their misunderstandings of what it was supposed to be, was very difficult."

But Tim refused to be discouraged. He continued to demonstrate the Web and to discuss it with colleagues during coffee breaks. He knew he was making slow but steady progress. To make the Web more attractive, Tim and Robert put more information on the server they had installed on Tim's NeXT computer. Tim had already provided the World Wide Web browser software to the CERN scientists who used NeXT computers. That enabled them to access all the new material. They could also write their own hypertext pages to share with one another.

But most people at CERN didn't have NeXT computers. Nicola Pellow helped Tim create a browser that would work on other computers. People at CERN who had NeXT computers could use the original browser to read and write Web pages. People who did not have NeXT computers could use Nicola's browser to read Web pages but not to write them.

Successful Demonstration

In May 1991, Tim learned that a physicist named Paul Kunz from Stanford University in Palo Alto, California, was visiting CERN. Calling Paul on the phone, Tim offered to show him what the Web could do. Paul didn't especially want to see a demonstration, but Tim was a good talker. He wouldn't take no for an answer. Paul expected to be bored. Instead, he grew excited when Tim showed him the way computers at CERN could communicate. But Paul wanted even more proof of the Web's power. Could Tim also access information on a computer located miles away? Paul wanted to know.

Conveniently, Paul had a NeXT computer in California. Over the Internet, Tim sent a copy of his browser software to Paul's computer. Within seconds, Paul saw information from his computer in California on Tim's computer at CERN. Paul was stunned. When Paul returned to Stanford, he arranged for his physics group to access the Web. They were so impressed that Stanford soon created the first Web page in the United States.

Remembering the day: Paul Kunz sets up the NeXT computer that he used to create the first U.S. Web page in celebration of its tenth anniversary.

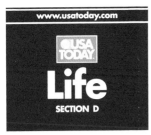

www.usatoday.com

USA TODAY

Life

SECTION D

December 11, 2001

First U.S. Web page went up 10 years ago

From the Pages of USA TODAY

It's hard to imagine what might have happened with the Web if Paul Kunz had skipped a meeting in Switzerland 10 years ago.

Wednesday marks the 10th anniversary of the first U.S. Web page, created by Kunz, a physicist at the Stanford Linear Accelerator Center (SLAC). He says that if World Wide Web creator Tim Berners-Lee hadn't insisted on the meeting, the Web wouldn't have taken off when it did—maybe not at all.

Kunz had heard about Berners-Lee's Web project, but frankly, "I wasn't very interested," he says. After all, the Internet and e-mail were already standard among scientists. The Web made it possible to graphically link to documents on other computers, but it was hard to imagine the implications.

Kunz, who was meeting with various scientists at CERN, the European Organization for Nuclear Research, grudgingly agreed to a 3 P.M. meeting.

By 6, Kunz was sold on the Web. The two scientists linked a computer near Geneva to one at SLAC. It was the first time that the Web was on the Internet.

Kunz went home and created what was to become the first Web page on a U.S. computer; it gave scientists easy access to SLAC's database of physics papers.

The page went up at 4 P.M. on Dec. 12, 1991. A month later at a conference in France, Berners-Lee clicked over the Kunz's Web page and searched the database. The scientists were sold.

"It was a very dramatic moment," Kunz says. "I realized without that last piece in the demo people would have forgotten about the Web before they got home." Instead, they went home and told all their colleagues. Then they started creating their own pages, and the rest, as they say, is history.

—Janet Kornblum, December 11, 2001

The Web Goes Worldwide

Tim worked hard to make the Web as easy to use on other kinds of computers as it was to use on the NeXT. On August 6, 1991, he took a bold step. He posted three key items on the Internet: 1) the World Wide Web software for NeXT computer editors, 2) a browser, and 3) a basic server that could be used with all computers. Before this date, only researchers in physics knew about the Web. With the three items Tim posted, anyone with a NeXT computer and Internet access could investigate what the Web was all about. As the British Broadcasting Corporation (BBC) would later put it, August 6, 1991, was the "day the Web went worldwide."

Internet users in colleges and scientific institutes took note. They e-mailed Tim with all sorts of suggestions, ideas, and general encouragement. They also told Tim of the problems they encountered in trying to use the Web. But the best e-mails of all came from those who had established their own Web pages. New websites were being created, and hypertext links were being forged. As Tim has remarked, "The people of the Internet built the Web, in true grass-roots fashion."

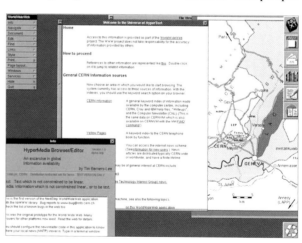

Finding a way: This screen shot shows the original Web browser Tim developed at CERN in 1991. The map shows the area around CERN, and the other windows give more information about navigating the World Wide Web.

"Slow Explosion"

Tim couldn't have been happier. To further promote the Web, he opened a public web server on his CERN computer. This became known as info.cern.ch. By accessing info.cern.ch, curious computer users would be automatically connected to a browser. With this connection, millions of people who didn't have NeXT computers could access the Web. But that wasn't all. The home page that came up from CERN's server would tell a user how to download a browser for individual use. Once again, Tim's strategy paid off. New Web servers and websites sprang up daily. "A slow explosion," is how Tim would later describe the phenomenon.

Hypertext Conference

Although the Web was for everyone, Tim felt one group would be especially interested in his work. These were people who were already using hypertext on their own computers. A big conference of hypertext users was being held in December 1991 in San Antonio, Texas. Hurriedly, Tim and Robert prepared a paper to present at the conference. To their disappointment, the conference officials rejected it, perhaps because it was so different from what they expected. Most hypertext users weren't plugged into the Web yet.

Tim and Robert attended the conference anyway. Lugging Tim's NeXT computer to Texas, they planned to give a simple demonstration of the Web. Several obstacles stood in their way. First, they needed a telephone outlet to hook up their modem, a device that allows computers to access the Internet through telephone lines. But there were no phone lines in the conference hall. On top of that, the Swiss modem they brought with them would not work with the U.S. electric system. They had to dismantle the modem, rewire it, and put it together with a soldering iron. Then they still needed a way for the modem to get Internet access.

Even after solving their problems, Tim and Robert found that the people who stopped to see their demonstration didn't seem to grasp the importance of the Web. Surprisingly few people could imagine that Tim's information system would really connect the globe. "They have chutzpah [boldness] in calling that the World Wide Web!" a conference attendee declared.

Many New Browsers

By this time, Tim was used to skepticism. And there was plenty of good news to balance his disappointment in Texas. Insightful individuals were beginning to recognize the Web as something powerful, practical, and utterly revolutionary. Knowledgeable college students were beginning to create browsers that worked on different computers. Tim welcomed this development. At Helsinki University of Technology in Finland, a group of young computer programmers created Erwise, a browser for UNIX computers. Pei Wei, a graduate student at the University of California at Berkeley, developed a browser called ViolaWWW that also worked for UNIX machines. Meanwhile, at CERN,

IN F⊕CUS

Broken Links

Before the World Wide Web, hypertext links were always reciprocal, or two-sided. In Tim's system, the links between two documents do not have to go both ways. For example, a website about endangered animal species might have a link to the famous zoo in San Diego, California. But if someone went to the San Diego Zoo website first, that person might not find a link back to the endangered species site.

This means a computer user might try to access a website that has been deleted or moved. This is called a broken link. Although Tim doesn't like broken links, he sees no way around them. To avoid broken links, all websites would have to be stored on a central computer. But that would limit the size of the Web.

www.usatoday.com

USA TODAY

Money
SECTION B

April 30, 2007

TOP 25: 25 years of paving the information superhighway

<u>From the Pages of</u>
<u>USA TODAY</u>

In 1982, PCs [personal computers] were connected to little more than dot-matrix printers. Owners soon hooked them to each other—and a little-known academic network called the Internet. A phenomenon was born. On its 25th anniversary USA TODAY chose events that turned the Net into the tool it is today.

1. World Wide Web
Tim Berners-Lee created user-friendly "Web pages" that could travel over the Internet, a network built to shuttle research between universities. The world logged on: 747 million adults in January.

2. E-mail
Tech's answer to the Pony Express. Programs such as 1988's Eudora made it easy to use. Inboxes have been filling up ever since. Nearly 97 billion e-mails are sent each day.

3. Graphical user interface (GUI)
Most computer displays were blinking lines of text until Apple featured clickable icons and other graphic tools in its 1984 Mac. Microsoft's Windows took GUI, pronounced "gooey," to the masses.

—April 30, 2007

Robert and some of Tim's other colleagues collaborated on a browser for Macintosh computers. They called their browser Samba.

On one hand, Tim felt encouraged. More browsers meant more people using the Web. But Tim was also a little disappointed. The new browsers allowed people to read what was posted on the Web but not to write or to edit Web content on their computers. Tim had envisioned that the writing and editing would be as easy as the reading.

Constantly busy, Tim continued to work on programs for CERN's new particle accelerator and to write new Web pages. Whenever possible, he took time off to attend computer conferences.

June 17, 1997

History takes on Net proportions.
The masters and prized artifacts now showing on line

From the Pages of
USA TODAY

The massive movement to digitize museum and library collections is letting on-line browsers get up close and personal with artwork and artifacts too precious and vulnerable for actual exhibition.

Hundreds of museums and galleries are on the Web. Later this summer, the Holdings project (Holding Our Library Documents Insures Nobility, Greatness and Strength) will offer on-line viewers a taste of the largest ongoing initiative to document the African American experience.

—Carol Memmott, June 17, 1997

Because Tim created the WWW using CERN's resources, the organization owned the property rights to the World Wide Web. CERN could have tried to charge a fee for anyone using the Web. But the officials at CERN had never been in a position to commercialize an invention before. They weren't sure how to handle the situation. The increase in new browsers added to the concern some people were feeling. As the Web expanded, they felt CERN should receive more credit.

Virtual Visit

New servers, browsers, and websites were popping up all over the place. As Tim pulled up new websites on his computer, he discovered a wealth of information. One site that especially intrigued Tim presented information about Rome during the Renaissance of the 1500s and 1600s. Entering a "virtual museum," Tim was delighted with the intricacy and beauty of the images. A richly decorated musical score that had been presented to Pope Clement VII especially delighted him. "I . . . was glad I had a twenty-one inch color screen," he later wrote. Tim never knew what surprises he would find on the Web next. His creation had taken on a life of its own.

Visiting: Tim visited the University of California at Berkeley (*above*) in 1992 to discuss the World Wide Web with Viola creator Pei Wei.

Browsing the Web

■■■■

The summer of 1992 found Tim traveling in the United States with his wife and daughter. After attending meetings in Boston, Massachusetts, and enjoying a family vacation, the Berners-Lees set off for San Francisco, California. Tim wanted to visit some people. He met with Paul Kunz, who had been so impressed by Tim's demonstration at CERN. And he stopped by the University of California at Berkeley to chat with Pei Wei, creator of the Viola browser.

At Stanford he called on Tony Johnson, the architect of another browser called Midas. Tim couldn't convince either Wei or Johnson to add writing functions to their browsers. But he loved exchanging ideas with people who shared his enthusiasm for the Web.

The Man Who Invented Hypertext

All summer Tim had looked forward to meeting Ted Nelson, the man who had invented hypertext and coined the name more than twenty years earlier. Ever since he learned of Ted's work, Tim had known he was a kindred spirit. Like Tim, Ted wanted to make it easier for people to publish and access all sorts of information online. Tim felt he owed a great deal to Ted.

Full of anticipation, Tim arrived at Ted's houseboat in Sausalito, California. His mood saddened when Ted shared some news. That same day, a major software company had abandoned plans to work with Xanadu, Ted's long-cherished hypertext project. Despite the disappointment, Tim and Ted had a good talk over lunch at an Indian restaurant. Each man wanted a souvenir of their special meeting. Tim took a photo of Ted for his scrapbook, and Ted took a video of Tim. Looking back on that summer, Tim described it as "a thrilling time."

Rapid Growth

The Web was taking off in the academic community. In a single year, the number of people using the Web had increased tenfold. Fifty servers were up and running by the beginning of 1993. That meant that fifty computers held thousands of Web pages that could be accessed anywhere in the world. Computer engineers were also developing new browsers, some with special features. Many of these browsers were made available to the public over the Internet.

Mosaic

In February 1993, Tim downloaded a new browser onto his computer at CERN. Called Mosaic, the browser had been created by a team of developers at the National Center for Supercomputing Applications (NCSA), located at the University of Illinois at Urbana-Champaign. Tim found the new browser easy to use. With a simple click, he could pull up anything he wanted from the Web.

Others appreciated Mosaic's convenience too. Tens of thousands of people downloaded it, making it perhaps the most popular browser at the time. As exciting as this was, Tim saw a possible danger. It seemed to him that the creators of Mosaic were promoting it as an alternative to the Web. Tim realized this could be confusing to general computer users. But he didn't dwell on his concerns. The development of Mosaic was a major accomplishment. Wasn't it only natural that those responsible should play it up as much as possible?

On another visit to the United States, he encouraged Marc Andreessen, Mosaic's lead developer, and his colleagues to incorporate a writing function into the browser. Tim still thought it was important for people to be able to create Web pages as easily as they read them. The people at NCSA disagreed. As the Web grew, software developers seemed more interested in getting graphics and colors on their browsers than in allowing users to edit the material. The fancy presentation generated a great deal of publicity.

The Web Expands

Back home in Geneva, Tim thought a great deal about the goals of NCSA. How would their efforts to promote Mosaic impact the World Wide Web? An article that appeared in the *New York Times* in 1993 especially bothered Tim. Spotlighting Mosaic, the article made no distinction between the popular browser and the Web itself. But a browser like Mosaic was only a tool that allowed users to access the Web. The World Wide Web is a vast network of information with all content accessible through unique URLs. How were readers to know this?

www.usatoday.com

USA TODAY

Money

SECTION B

August 10, 1995

Andreessen: 'Vanguard' of new entrepreneurs

<u>From the Pages of USA TODAY</u>

Marc Andreessen, 24, co-founder of Netscape, owns shares and options worth $58 million Wednesday. . . . Today, Andreessen's Netscape is Wall Street's darling and the hottest new high-tech company.

Andreesseen, the 6-foot-5 idea man, is often referred to as the next Bill Gates. But Andreessen had a vision that eluded even Microsoft's co-founder and CEO. That vision was the future of the Internet. He and colleagues developed software, "Mosaic," to allow users to point and click their way around the World Wide Web, the Internet section where text, photo and sound coexist.

"I was skeptical," says Mosaic co-creator Eric Bina, who now works at Netscape. "But it took off like nobody believed."

—Julie Schmit,
August 10, 1995

Marc Andreessen

Tim knew he had to do something. As more new browsers were becoming available, Tim wanted to ensure that each one would be able to access all the material on the Web. It would defeat the purpose of the Web, he thought, if different browsers were needed to access different kinds of information. For example, a company might put a great deal of material on the Web that would be relevant to the general public. That same company might make the material accessible only through a specific browser. If several groups did this, the Web would become fragmented. Tim did not want the Web to "splinter into various factions—some commercial, some academic; some free, some not." From the very beginning, he had always meant it to be the free exchange of information.

Meanwhile, the Web continued to grow by leaps and bounds. Tim liked to monitor its progress by checking on the number of people who visited the CERN Web server every day. By the summer

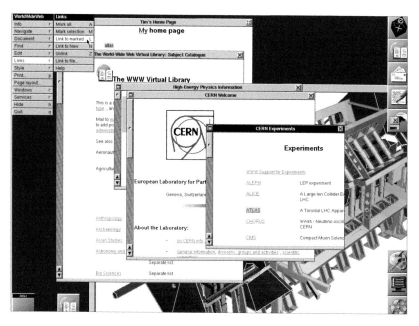

Browsing: This screen shot shows Tim's Web browser in use in 1993. Many Web browsers were developed in the early 1990s.

of 1993, this amounted to ten thousand hits per day. People began to depend on the Web for fast, accurate information on a variety of topics.

But the tremendous growth of the Web also posed a problem for Tim. CERN had never charged any fees when someone put up a new browser or server. It collected no royalties (payment) when someone created software that used the special World Wide Web code. Tim was anxious to keep it that way.

Gopher

If CERN ever decided to collect fees, Tim feared it would suffer the same fate as another information system called Gopher. Gopher had been developed at the University of Minnesota. In some ways, it was similar to the World Wide Web. The two systems coexisted for a while, competing for users. Then officials at the university decided to charge people for the privilege of using Gopher. Only nonprofit organizations and schools could use Gopher for free.

That was the end of Gopher's popularity! Almost everyone stopped using it. People stopped creating browsers, or software, for fear they would be sued. When Tim attended a meeting in Ohio, people complained about what the University of Minnesota had done. "Is CERN going to do the same thing with WWW?" they demanded. Tim couldn't answer that question for certain. Although he acted unruffled, inside he was a nervous wreck.

 The University of Minnesota, as well as a few other places, still has facilities for accessing Gopher. But most of the material once available on Gopher has been rewritten into HTML and posted on the World Wide Web.

Public Domain

For more than a year, Tim and Robert had been trying to convince officials at CERN to officially give up their legal rights to WWW. When Tim returned to Geneva, they became more insistent in his requests. He wanted everything connected with the Web to be placed in the public domain (as free community property). That way everyone could use the Web for free, without worry that they were infringing on someone else's rights. Tim continued to be very concerned until April 30, 1993. That day an official CERN document arrived addressed to Tim and to Robert Cailliau. Tim's request had been granted! Everyone would be allowed to put up a server or create a browser free of charge. Tim later summed up his feelings with a single word. "Whew!"

Protecting the Web

One problem was solved, but Tim was still anxious about the future of the Web. There was still the possibility that it could splinter into different groups. And what if a single institute or company gained control over the Web by promoting a particular browser as the best way to explore it? Tim did not want any one organization to dictate policy. He began to think about creating a consortium—that is, an organization of businesses and agencies whose main purpose would be to safeguard the well-being of the Web.

Tim had already discussed the idea with others. "Commercial, educational, and government bodies are all rushing to get on board," he wrote in a note to himself. "[They] are calling for a central body to define the Web, ensure its stability and smooth progression through continued technological innovation." Tim envisioned an organization that would hash out problems and make recommendations for the best functioning of the Web. It would encourage people all over the world, from all walks of life and all economic levels, to explore the Web. Tim even hoped that a consortium would help less developed countries harness the power of the World Wide Web.

At last Tim was ready to act on his ideas. He knew he couldn't create a consortium on his own. He would need the backing of a powerful organization such as CERN. In October 1993, Tim presented CERN officials with a proposal for a consortium that would be centered at the famous physics facility. He knew it was a gamble. CERN was gearing up to build another particle accelerator, bigger and better than the previous one. Most of CERN's funding and resources would be used for that. Would officials at CERN feel they could sponsor the World Wide Web Consortium as well? Tim could only hope so. The future of the Web depended on it.

New horizons: Tim's life and landscape were about to change after a train ride through the Swiss mountains.

Heading the Consortium

Traveling by train through the Swiss mountains, Tim thought about his upcoming appointment. He still hadn't heard from CERN about his proposal for a consortium. For several months, he had been exchanging e-mails about his hopes with a man named Michael Dertouzos. A Greek immigrant to the United States, Michael served as director of Laboratory for Computer Sciences at the Massachusetts Institute of Technology (MIT) in Cambridge, Massachusetts. He often came to Europe to visit family and conduct business. Tim and Michael had arranged to meet in Zurich, Switzerland. Tim didn't know what to expect from their meeting, but he looked forward to it.

The two men met at a restaurant in an old section of the city. Soon Tim was speaking energetically, punctuating his words with dramatic gestures, as he talked about the Web and the possible consortium. Later, Michael recalled his own excitement as he listened. Tim compared the evolving Web to a "gigantic brain" that would help people clarify their ideas and would stimulate future thought. It was very similar to Michael's vision of what he called "the information market-place." The more the two men talked, the more Michael wanted to be part of Tim's plans. As they sipped coffee late that night, they began planning their partnership.

Wizards Workshop

One month later, an editor at a publishing company hosted a small meeting billed as "the first WWW Wizards Workshop" in Cambridge, Massachusetts. About twenty-five people already active on the Web gathered at the publisher's office just blocks from MIT. Tim enjoyed greeting friendly faces, hailing old acquaintances such as Tom Bruce and Pei Wei, and taking photos. It was a great opportunity for Tim to discuss his hopes for a consortium. In one session, Tim collected ideas for ensuring the progression of the Web. He wrote down all the comments on the whiteboards and sticky bits of paper that covered the walls. By the time the group was done, all four walls were covered with suggestions.

Tim had a lot to ponder on his return home. There were several paths he could have followed. He could have started his own software company. Or he might have studied for an advanced degree in computers and pursued an academic career. But neither alternative appealed to Tim. The future of the Web was more important to him than money.

Besides his regular work for CERN, he continued to monitor the Web's progress and to negotiate with Michael at MIT about a consortium. In his free time, he still liked to go hiking and climb mountains in the Alps. But Tim was happiest spending time with his wife and growing daughter. On warm days, they liked to eat dinner in the backyard overlooking the mountains.

Planning the Consortium

Nothing could be farther from the peace of Tim's little French village than the sprawling urban campus of MIT. Soon Tim returned to the bustle of Cambridge, Massachusetts, to talk with Michael Dertouzos. If they formed a consortium, where would it be located? Tim paused when Michael asked the question. MIT was sponsoring the Web, so the famous school would be the logical place to base the new organization. That was fine with Tim, but he didn't want to leave CERN out of the picture. He felt strongly that the new organization should have two bases—one in the United States and one in Europe. Michael heartily approved Tim's suggestion.

In May 1994, Tim and Nancy welcomed Al Vezza, an administrator from MIT, to Geneva. Al urged Tim to move to Massachusetts, and Tim saw the soundness of his reasoning. The Web was already more established in the United States than in Europe. Tim wanted to be in the very thick of Web activity—even if it meant leaving the mountainous countryside he had come to love. He also admired the spirit of adventure with which Americans tackle business and technological challenges. Yes, he told Al, he would be willing to come to the United States. As an added benefit, the move would allow Nancy to live much closer to her family.

First International Conference

So much needed to be done before Tim could begin his new venture. Shortly after Al's visit, Tim and Robert organized the First International World Wide Web Conference at CERN. Before the opening, Tim rushed around nonstop, trying to sort out last-minute conference details. Not everyone recognized Tim. When he tried to get into the conference area, student volunteers in charge of registration ordered him out. He was too early, they declared sternly. They were not supposed to let anyone enter yet. Tim had to do some fancy talking to convince them who he really was!

Once the conference did get going, Tim made some fascinating contacts. As he later said, "For the first time people who were developing the Web were brought together with all sorts of people who were using it in all sorts of ways." Together they hashed out some burning issues. How could Web servers keep pace when multiple requests for the same Web page arrived at the same time? How could mathematical tables and photographs be most easily embedded in HTML? Participants were passionate about such questions. Enthusiasm ran so high that news reporters compared the event to Woodstock, a famous U.S. rock concert of the 1960s.

When Tim stood up to make some closing remarks, however, he felt nervous. He wanted to underscore the moral and ethical responsibility of everyone helping to create the Web. But how would people react to his message? Would they think he was being too preachy? Tim felt the matter was too important to ignore. He forced himself to speak his mind. Instead of the negative response he feared, the participants expressed warm acceptance of his words.

Relaxing, Tim moved on to the part of his speech he knew would excite everyone. Most of the details had been worked out between MIT and CERN for the creation of the World Wide Web Consortium. It was still too early to make an official announcement, but Tim felt a very broad hint was in order. He declared that there would be a special organization to help steer the Web's growth. "It's going to be a meeting point," he continued. "It's going to be a center for stability. But it'll never be able to do all the development, of course, and it wouldn't want to. So it's going to be a place where institutes and companies meet." Tim went on to explain the partnership between MIT and CERN. "So that's the W3 [WWW] Organization un-announcement," he finished his comments, "and that wraps up my talk for today."

The applause was deafening. But once more, there was excitement at home too. In June, Tim and Nancy's second child, Ben, was born. Happily Tim helped his wife care for their two children. For Tim, family would always come first.

Hectic Move

Soon after Ben's birth, Tim got the call he had been expecting. The final details at MIT had been worked out. The World Wide Web Consortium was a reality at last. On September 1, only six weeks away, he would begin his new responsibilities at MIT as director of the consortium.

Meanwhile, Tim and Nancy had planned to take their children on a vacation. As they prepared for their holiday, they couldn't be certain they would have time to return to their Swiss home before moving to the United States. It seemed wise to take along as many toys, clothes, personal papers, and other necessities as possible. When they were done packing, they had sixteen crates and boxes. Tim and Nancy's friends had to pitch in to help them get to the airport. Laden with luggage, the family set off on a wonderful vacation.

Adjusting to MIT

Tim and Nancy soon found a house to rent in Boston, but Tim didn't have time to buy a car before reporting to work. Every morning he took the bus to MIT, enjoying the bright colors of the autumn leaves. His temporary workspace was simply a desk in a windowless storage area. But Tim didn't mind. Michael Dertouzos and Al Vezza had offices nearby. It was easy to get together and make plans for the consortium.

Contributors: Michael Dertouzos *(left),* an MIT computer scientist, helped Tim form the World Wide Web Consortium and worked out the details to house the consortium on the MIT campus in Cambridge, Massachusetts.

IN FOCUS

New Spaces

Tim graduated from the storage area to his own office at MIT in the mid-1990s. About ten years later, he moved to the newly completed Stata Center, which houses the Computer Science and Artificial Intelligence Laboratory (CSAIL) of which W3C is a part. Designed by noted architect Frank Gehry, the innovative structure combines interesting angles, towers, cubes, cylinders, and diverse building materials in surprising ways. Tim took a keen interest in the building while it was still in the planning stages. The windows of most tall buildings remain permanently shut, and Tim was eager for windows that could open. To his delight, they do. "It's fun to have a building with such complicated shapes," says Tim. "The walls are so crinkled it's as if everyone has a corner office."

Innovative design: In the early twenty-first century, Tim got another new office in the Computer Science and Artificial Intelligence Lab at MIT's Stata Center *(above)*.

New office: Tim stands in his new office at MIT in 1995.

On December 14, Tim led the first gathering of the consortium's advisory committee. Emphasizing the openness of the Web, Tim said it would not have a central headquarters. Anyone could put up a server or create a new browser without approval from the consortium.

Tim was hardly settled at MIT when Netscape Communications, the company founded by Marc Andreessen, announced the creation of a new browser. Named Mozilla, the browser could be used with many popular home computers. Anyone could download it for free. Mozilla gave a whole new audience access to the Web, causing the Web to grow by leaps and bounds.

IN FOCUS

The Personal Computer

Before the 1970s, only large companies, universities, and governments had access to computers. When microprocessors became available in 1972, small computers for home use became an affordable reality. Three years later, in January 1975, a failing electronics company named MITS advertised what has been called "the first 'personal' computer." Thousands of orders poured in, saving the company from bankruptcy. Other companies were eager to join the bandwagon. The Apple II home computer arrived on the market in 1977. Developed by Steve Jobs and Steve Wozniak in Silicon Valley, California, the Apple II was billed as "the computer that's ready to work, play, and grow with you." Personal computers, or PCs, developed at an incredible rate. As they acquired more applications and memory and as the cost got lower, the public rushed to buy them. The personal computer revolution had begun.

New Centers

Two days after the meeting, Tim received disappointing news. CERN could no longer be part of the consortium. The center had just committed itself to building the new particle accelerator. All CERN's funds and resources would be channeled into this gigantic undertaking. Nothing would be left over to contribute to the growth of the Web. Although Tim understood the wisdom of CERN's decision, he also felt a deep sadness. He cherished his time at CERN. The institute had given him the time, space, and freedom to create the World Wide Web. "I would rather have seen the organization get a pat on the back than go quietly into the night," he later wrote.

Tim didn't have to look far to find another European base for the consortium. The Institut National de Recherche en Informatique et en Automatique (INRIA) in France was a famous national institute for computer research and communications. Already involved with the

Web, the institute's scientists had created a browser that could also edit hypertext pages. That was a project dear to Tim's heart! He still hoped that someday most browsers would allow their users to write as well as read in hypertext.

Immediately Tim got in touch with officials at INRIA. When he broached the idea of their becoming the European anchor of the consortium in 1995, they were happy to agree. Later, so many companies from Japan and Asia joined the consortium that it needed a base in the Far East as well. In 1996 Keio University in Japan accepted the responsibility.

New partner: INRIA, the National Institute for Computer Research, in France agreed to take over CERN's place in the consortium in 1995.

On January 1, 2003, INRIA passed along its role as the European host of the World Wide Web Consortium to another organization in France—the European Research Consortium for Informatics and Mathematics (ERCIM). By this time, almost 450 organizations belonged to the consortium. "With the move to ERCIM, there is the potential for considerable growth and synergies of Web technologies across Europe," announced Tim Berners-Lee.

Already wildly successful, the World Wide Web was poised to take off beyond most people's imagination. This was exactly what Tim had hoped for. When he first made the Web software available for general use in 1991, only about 600,000 people were using the Internet. By 1996 that number had skyrocketed to an estimated 40 million. People couldn't get enough of the World Wide Web. Individuals with advanced computer

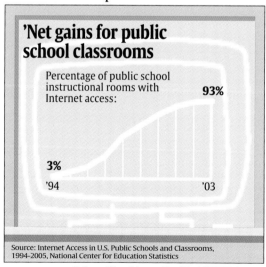

USA TODAY Snapshots®

'Net gains for public school classrooms

Percentage of public school instructional rooms with Internet access:

93%

3%

'94   '03

Source: Internet Access in U.S. Public Schools and Classrooms, 1994-2005, National Center for Education Statistics

By Tracey Wong Briggs and Sam Ward, USA TODAY, 2007

November 3, 1999

Top Technologists

From the Pages of **USA TODAY**

According to Opinion Research for CNET and Techies.com, when asked to choose the "top three technologists of this century," American adults picked: Bill Gates (48%); Henry Ford (46%); Wilbur and Orville Wright (41%); John Mauchly (38%); Gugliemo Marconi (38%); Tim Berners-Lee (25%); Ben Logan Baird (23%); and Steve Jobs (14%).

—Anonymous, November 3, 1999

skills could write their own Web pages and help others to do so. Even Tim hadn't anticipated such rapid growth. He was surprised by the number of people prepared to learn HTML. Businesses, schools, and other organizations started posting information on the Web. Colors and animation added to the excitement.

A Church Like the Web

As Tim and Nancy adjusted to their new home, they began to think of establishing spiritual roots for their children. They decided to visit every church in their neighborhood in an effort to find the one that was right for them. The first one they tried happened to be a Unitarian Universalist church. Tim liked the minister's style and message. She encouraged people to think creatively and exchange ideas in an atmosphere of tolerance and respect. These were Tim's goals for the Web too. Tim and Nancy abandoned their plans to explore other churches. They had found a place where they felt comfortable and welcome.

Cleaning up: Student use of the Internet and the Web led to concerns about what was available on the Web during the mid-1990s.

Machines Talking to Machines

Tim's work was never predictable. As the Web grew, so did the World Wide Web Consortium. "We never knew when it would be a quiet day or when the phone would be ringing off the hook," Tim recalled. Soon he faced an extremely sensitive issue. John Patrick, an early member of the consortium, was worried about offensive or indecent materials on the Web. The company he worked for, IBM, wanted all students to have Internet access at school.

Many parents and teachers opposed the idea, John explained. They didn't want their children to be exposed to inappropriate content.

Fighting Censorship

The consortium didn't want to impose censorship on the Web. They felt that would be a terrible blow to freedom of speech. But John wouldn't budge. "Something has to be done," he insisted, "or children won't be given access to the Web."

Meanwhile, the U.S. Congress was considering legislation that would specify what types of materials were appropriate for the Web. This was a kind of censorship. The consortium needed to act quickly to give parents an alternative to such legislation. Pooling their efforts, the member companies came up with a system to help adults evaluate websites. Parents would receive descriptions of websites along with special software. The language for describing the content was called the Platform for Internet Content Selection (PICS). Using the PICS software, parents could block sites that they did not want their children to see.

USA TODAY Snapshots®

Stopping improper materials

Percentage of public schools with procedures to prevent students from accessing inappropriate material on the Internet:

Monitoring by teachers or other staff
2001 — 91%
2005 — 96%

Blocking/ filtering software
2001 — 87%
2005 — 99%

Source: Department of Education

By David Stuckey and Robert W. Ahrens, USA TODAY, 2006

But Congress moved faster than the consortium. On February 8, 1996, President Bill Clinton signed the Communications Decency Act of 1996 into law. One month later, the consortium released its software to the public. As a result, Tim was asked to appear on a news program.

At his local television studio, a very nervous Tim sat alone in a small room. The interviewer, who was located elsewhere, would communicate with Tim via satellite. A camera would broadcast Tim's face to home viewers as he answered questions. The minutes were ticking down to Tim's appearance. Then he heard the voice of the interviewer, "We'll be back in a few minutes with Tim Berners-Lee and his plans to control the Internet."

Tim's anxiety level shot through the roof. He had never said anything about controlling the Internet! Several minutes later, he heard the interviewer's voice again. "Well, Tim Berners-Lee, so you actually invented the World Wide Web. Tell us, exactly how rich are you?" The question, which Tim found ridiculous, caught him off guard. He could scarcely get his words out. And because Tim was at a loss for words, the television crew shortened the interview to get him off the air quickly.

Later that year, the U.S. Supreme Court declared the Communications Decency Act to be unconstitutional because it violated the First Amendment right of free speech. The fact that parents could use the PICS and other new software filtering packages to protect their children was an important factor in the justices' decision. The legislation, lawyers argued, wasn't needed.

Semantic Web

The World Wide Web had added a creative new dimension to business and education. People went to the Web for information on everything from buying a dog to researching an illness to learning more about world events. But Tim has always felt that the Web was only half done. For several years, he has been working on what he calls the Semantic Web. This second stage of Tim's invention allows computers to make correlations between pieces of information on the Web. The original Web is good for reading documents but not as good for analyzing data such as spreadsheets, calendars, bank statements, and address books. The Semantic Web will help people to analyze such data files from many different points of view.

"A human being browse the Web?" Tim laughed in a recent interview. "That will be a little old-fashioned." On their own, computers will be able to conduct business and sift through data for material. Data files with links between websites will help computers do this.

Plans: Tim stands in front of a chalkboard with his notes on Web development in the late 1990s.

They will be able to process the connections between different sets of data. To put it simply, machines will be talking to machines.

Computers still won't be able to "think" and make judgments as people do, but they will free people to focus on the more creative parts of a task. Tim gives a specific example of what the Semantic Web would do. Suppose a viral epidemic were to break out. Doctors would want to get all the information they could about the epidemic. Instead of having to search the Web for each piece of information, they could rely on the Semantic Web to gather all the information for them. The Semantic

October 1, 2004

Next big thing: The Web as your servant; What if the Web could anticipate your needs?

<u>From the Pages of</u>
<u>USA TODAY</u>

The Web is over. Now comes the next big thing, growing out of . . . wireless and wired networks, gadgets, software, satellites and social changes created over the past decade. . . .

Some in tech call it the world network. A big part of the promise is that it will turn the Web around: Instead of having to find information or entertainment, it will find you—and be exactly what you want or need at that moment. The network becomes a butler. . . .

What will the world network do for people? One example, culled from interviews with executives and entrepreneurs across the tech industry, might be a service

Web would reveal to doctors where the outbreaks occurred, how many casualties there were, what treatments were most effective, and what areas were best prepared to deal with the epidemic. The Semantic Web would match the locations of the outbreaks with the recovery rate and medical resources available in those areas. It would provide the ages and gender of the patients as well as risk factors for the disease. The analysis, which could take days or even weeks for researchers, would be speedy and accurate. It would help administrators and doctors develop a plan to quickly control the spread of the disease.

we'll call Travel Butler, or TB for short. It doesn't exist, but services like it are a gleam in the eye of companies ranging from Orbitz to AT&T.

Let's say it's 4 P.M. TB knows you have a flight scheduled for 6 P.M. because it regularly prowls the Web sites you use for travel and found you booked a ticket on Orbitz. TB can tell, perhaps by checking your online calendar, that you're at a meeting downtown.

The service cross-checks with a map service such as MapQuest to find the route you'd have to take to the airport. Once it knows that, TB goes out on the network to monitor traffic on your route—and finds the streams of data on the Department of Transportation Web site, which monitors road cameras and sensors.

TB might see that accidents have backed up traffic for miles. It sends you a message, which finds you on your BlackBerry e-mail, saying that to make your flight, you'd have to leave now. TB also shows you an Orbitz listing of later flights.

You decide to go on a later flight, so you click on the one you want. TB rebooks you, sends an e-mail to your spouse and contacts the car service in your destination city to change the time to pick you up. . . .

Web creator Tim Berners-Lee has been talking about a version of such a system for a couple of years. "The Web can reach its full potential only if it becomes a place where data can be shared and processed by automated tools as well as by people," Berners-Lee said Wednesday at the Massachusetts Institute of Technology.

—Kevin Maney, October 1, 2004

First Book

In the late 1990s, the number of people using the World Wide Web continued to soar. Less than ten years earlier, it hadn't even existed. To many people, it seemed as if the Web had simply burst onto the scene overnight. Where had it come from? Tim decided to answer that question by writing a book. In *Weaving the Web*, which he wrote with science writer and editor Mark Fischetti, Tim tells all about his days at CERN, his early struggles to promote the Web, and his dreams for the future. For Tim the Web was a way to bring people together, and no one must be left out. "We have to be careful that [the Web] allows for a just and fair society," he wrote. For Tim this means universal access. Regardless of income, politics, or physical or mental ability, everyone has to be able to use the Web. There should be no language or cultural barriers.

IN FOCUS

What Would You Add to the Web?

Can you imagine the world without the Web? In less than two decades, people have come to depend on the endless resources it provides. Cities, schools, businesses, historic landmarks, and government offices have websites. So do political candidates, authors, artists, musicians, professors, and other individuals. People use the Web in all sorts of ways to enrich and broaden their lives. Online universities give students a chance to earn a college degree without traveling to a distant city. Bargain hunters can find just the purchase they want. Blogs give individuals a chance to express their views. Search engines allow people to research anything from the job market to how to grow a better tomato. And there's more to come. "The Web is not done," Tim declares. "What we have imagined will pale before what is to come. Speaking especially to young people, he asks, "Can you think of something you'd love the Web to have which it does not have? Maybe you will add it yourself."

www.usatoday.com

USA TODAY

Money

SECTION B

October 20, 1999

Inventor of Web weaves tale of its past, present, future

<u>From the Pages of</u>
<u>USA TODAY</u>

ARLINGTON, Va.—The inventor of the World Wide Web, Tim Berners-Lee, is headed to USA TODAY....

So the elevator dings and out walks ... out walks a cute, young-looking Brit with a mischievous sparkle in his eye, blond hair that kind of sticks up in front, and a tendency to mutter a lot of non sequiturs [unconnected ideas] under his breath in the peculiarly British way. He's wearing a tie that's a scene from an impressionist painting. He's funny and likable and about as intimidating as the Pikachu runt from my kids' Pokemon collection.

He shows up carrying one thing: a digital camera. He takes pictures of me and of the photographer taking his picture. He takes pictures of everyone he meets and pastes them in a digital scrapbook.

He seems to like the title Inventor of the World Wide Web. He bears it confidently, the way Joe DiMaggio bore Greatest Living Ballplayer. But he's not in your face with it. In fact, Berners-Lee, who never courted fame and never sought fortune from his baby, sometimes finds his icon status a bit strange.

"When I meet someone at a party, I don't know if the person wanted to meet me or meet the inventor of the World Wide Web," he says. "I don't like that aspect—that you get treated differently."

He has never founded a dot-com company. Never became an instant ... billionaire. It simply was never in his plan to cash in—something lots of people, especially Americans, find ludicrous, he says.

His real job lately has been director of the World Wide Web Consortium, the closest thing to a governing body for the Internet. That job is starting to take him back toward research and inventing, as he tries to use the consortium to push the Web toward the next steps ...

—Kevin Maney, October 20, 1999

Tim does not want complicated procedures or technology to stand in the way of anyone creating websites or sharing ideas. Looking to the future, he "would like it to be easier for ordinary people to be creative on the Web and to be creative in groups on the Web."

Honors

The twentieth century was winding down when Tim published his book in 1999. That same year, *Time* magazine listed him as one of the "Time 100"—one of the 100 greatest minds of the century. Tim had received many awards in the past few years, including the Kilby International Awards Foundation's "Young Innovator of the Year" Award, a Columbus Prize from the International Communication Institute, and a Lifetime Achievement Award in Technical Excellence from *PC Magazine*. But the *Time* magazine honor did more than any other to make more people aware of him. As usual, Tim's excitement spilled over into

Life to paper: Tim holds his book *Weaving the Web* during a photo shoot while promoting the book.

enthusiastic gestures and galloping speech when he talked with reporters about the Web. Asked more personal questions, Tim slowed down a great deal. He felt a strong need to protect his family's privacy. "Work is work, and home is home," he explained politely but firmly.

Work for Tim means monitoring hundreds of projects for the consortium. These include the development of new software and the promotion of policies to keep the Web free and open to everyone. He also pursues his work on the Semantic Web.

When he has some free time, Tim still likes to hike, run, and ski. Sometimes as he jogs on a wintry New England morning, he can almost imagine himself back in snowy Geneva. The outdoors has always been a source of inspiration to Tim. What would he do if he had millions of

IN F⊙CUS

Heady Company

Time magazine divided its 1999 list of the 100 greatest minds of the twentieth century into five categories. In the "Scientists and Thinkers" category, Tim shared the spotlight with such notables as Wilbur and Orville Wright, who made the first flight in a heavier-than-air flying machine; Enrico Fermi, whose work led to the creation of the first atomic bomb; and the person-of-the-century, Albert Einstein.

Great mind: Albert Einstein in 1931

dollars? a reporter once wanted to know. After some thought, Tim replied that he would buy a piece of land that was being threatened by building developers. He envisioned clearing away commercial structures and inviting the public to enjoy unspoiled nature.

In 2003 Tim became a Fellow in the Royal Society, England's national academy of science. As part of the induction ceremony, Tim had to sign his name in the Register of Fellows. Looking through the book prior to writing his signature, he was thrilled to see the handwriting of Sir Isaac Newton, one of the greatest scientists who ever lived.

Sir Timothy

The week after his forty-ninth birthday, Tim went to Helsinki, Finland, to accept the first Millennium Technology Prize ever awarded. The very next month, Tim and his family were in London for the event of a lifetime. Tim was being knighted by Great Britain's Queen Elizabeth II. Recalling his visit inside the fence around Buckingham Palace, the royal residence in London, he remarked, "It's about as much of a shock to go through the railings as it is to go through the mirror like Alice in Wonderland." After the queen dubbed him with her father's sword, Tim left the palace as Sir Timothy. Often described as "famously modest," Tim made sure reporters knew that many people were responsible for the growth of the Web.

Recognition and honors kept coming to Tim. He was declared Greatest Briton 2004. That same year, he took a part-time position in the Computer Science Department at the University of Southampton in England. In 2008 MIT awarded Tim the 3Com Founders Professorship of Engineering.

Celebration: Tim *(right)* receives the Millenium Technology Prize from the president of Finland in 2004.

Tim believes that one of the most important accomplishments of the Web is that individuals are able to work together, sometimes connecting over vast distances, to inspire creativity in one another. He believes such cooperation leads to an increased tolerance and understanding among cultures and nations.

Tim's advice to students? "I think you should all be careful to spend as much time using the other parts of your brain as you do using a computer. Take a break and do a little calligraphy to let your thoughts settle. Keep a musical instrument within reach of your computer at home." Tim himself enjoys playing the piano and the guitar, though he calls himself strictly an "amateur."

Looking to the future, Tim expects the Web to get "better and better." He thinks it will become available almost everywhere, with computer screens on "walls, automobile dashboards, and refrigerator doors. From the beginning," says Tim, "there were people all over the world who had the imagination to see what the Web could be. That spirit of excitement is on the Web today."

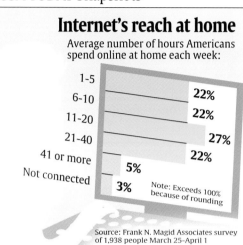

USA TODAY Snapshots®

Internet's reach at home

Average number of hours Americans spend online at home each week:

1-5	
6-10	22%
11-20	22%
21-40	27%
41 or more	22%
	5%
Not connected	3%

Note: Exceeds 100% because of rounding

Source: Frank N. Magid Associates survey of 1,938 people March 25-April 1

By Anne R. Carey and Sam Ward, USA TODAY, 2008

IN FOCUS

New Foundation

In September 2008, Tim announced plans to create the World Wide Web Foundation "to ensure the Web serves humanity as well as it can." The foundation will further the work of the consortium "in developing Web standards and supporting research into how the Web can be better."[7] In addition, the foundation will study how to help people who can't yet access the Web. As of 2008, approximately 20 percent of the world's population can use the Web. That number is not nearly good enough for Tim. Through his foundation, Tim plans to make it easier for people all over the world to get online. He wants to explore ways to make the Web accessible to people who can't read or write. And he wants to ensure no one government or company has too much control over the Web.

GLOSSARY

browser: software that allows a computer to access the World Wide Web

CERN: a famous facility for physics research located near Geneva, Switzerland

chip: a small, thin slice of a semiconducting material, usually silicon, that directs the workings of electronic devices; also called a microchip

European Research Consortium for Informatics and Mathematics (ERCIM): a French-based organization that serves as the European host of the World Wide Web Consortium

Gopher: an information system developed by the University of Minnesota 1991 that is similar in some ways to the World Wide Web. Gopher lost its popularity when certain classes of users were charged fees.

hypertext: a way to present text in which highlighted words and phrases are linked to other documents

Hypertext Markup Language (HTML): a text processing language that allows authors to link to other documents and data

Hypertext Transfer Protocol (HTTP): a set of procedures that allows one computer to transfer information to another computer

Internet: a network of networks that allows computers to send messages and documents to one another via cables

Keio University: Japanese university near Tokyo that serves as the Asian base of the World Wide Web Consortium

link: an Internet connection between two documents or Web pages

Massachusetts Institute of Technology (MIT): the university that serves as the U.S. base for the World Wide Web Consortium

microprocessor: small but exceptionally powerful computer chip that paved the way for personal computers

modem: a device that allows computers to exchange information over telephone lines

National Center for Supercomputing Applications (NCSA): a computer development group at the University of Illinois that created the popular Mosaic browser

National Institute for Research in Computer Science and Control (INRIA): a French computer research center that served as the second European base for the World Wide Web Consortium

node: a document or individual site on the World Wide Web

Remote Procedure Call (RPC): a procedure that allows a program on one computer to control what happens on other computers

Uniform Resource Locator (URL): a unique address assigned to every Web document

Web client: a computer that provides access to the World Wide Web but that does not store Web pages

Web server: a computer that stores Web pages, which are accessible to other computers

World Wide Web: a body of interconnected documents and Web pages that are accessible through the Internet

World Wide Web Consortium: a group that oversees the growth of the Web and develops standards and policies to keep the Web freely open to everyone

SOURCE NOTES

4   James Gillies and Robert Cailliau, *How the Web Was Born: The Story of the World Wide Web* (Oxford: Oxford University Press, 2000), 280.

5   Tim Berners-Lee, *Weaving the Web: The Original Design and Ultimate Destiny of the World Wide Web,* with Mark Fischetti (New York: HarperBusiness, 2000), 49.

6   Robert Wright, "The Man Who Invented the Web: Tim Berners-Lee Started a Revolution, but It Didn't Go Exactly As Planned," *Time*, May 19, 1997, http://www.chuckallan.com/fccj/cgs2555/tim-berners-lee.html (July 5, 2007).

7   Hilary Kahn and Brian Napper, "Manchester Celebrates the 50th Anniversary of the First Stored-Program Computer," *Computer 50*, 1998. http://www.computer50.org/mark1/ (August 1, 2008).

8   Tim Berners-Lee, telephone interview with author, January 16, 2008.

9   Nigel Farndale, "Tim Berners-Lee: A Very British Boffin," *Telegraph .co.uk*, March 30, 2008. http://www.telegraph.co.uk/connected/main .jhtml?xml=/connected/2008/03/30/sv_timbernerslee.xml&page=3 (July 15, 2008).

10 Leonard de Vries, *The Book of Experiments,* n.d., available online at http://www.vidyaonline.net/arvindgupta/bookofexpts.pdf (January 16, 2009).

15 Tim Berners-Lee, interviewed by Daniel S. Morrow, "Tim Berners-Lee Oral History," April 23, 2001, edited transcript of a video history interview, Cambridge, MA.

16 Ibid.

16 Ibid.

19 Tim Berners-Lee, telephone interview with author, August 28, 2008.

19 Ibid.

19 Berners-Lee, "Tim Berners-Lee Oral History."

20 Gillies and Cailliau, 155.

23 Berners-Lee with Fischetti, 8.

25 Gillies and Cailliau, 158.

26 Berners-Lee with Fischetti, 9.

26 Gillies and Cailliau, 170.

27 Berners-Lee with Fischetti, 4.

28   Bobbie Johnson, "The Guardian Profile: Tim Berners-Lee," *Guardian*, August 12, 2005. http://www.guardian.co.uk/technology/2005/aug/12/uknews.onlinesupplement (August 9, 2008).

30   Gillies and Cailliau, 172–173.

31   Berners-Lee with Fischetti, 12.

34   Tim Berners-Lee, "Frequently Asked Questions by the Press." *World Wide Web Consortium*, n.d., http://www.w3.org/People/Berners-Lee/FAQ.html (July 31, 2007).

35   Tim Berners-Lee, "Information Management: A Proposal," *CERN*, May 1990, http://www.nic.funet.fi/index/FUNET/history/internet/w3c/proposal.html (August 10, 2008).

38   Gillies and Cailliau, 180.

38   Ibid., 184.

39   Berners-Lee, interview with the author, January 16, 2008.

41   Ibid.

41   Ibid.

41   Colin Barker, "NeXT Computer: When Cool Wasn't Enough," *vnunet.com*, October 17, 2000. http://www.vnunet.com/vnunet/features/2129861/computer-wasn't-enough (August 9, 2008).

42   Gillies and Cailliau, 198.

44   Berners-Lee with Fischetti, 23.

50   Ibid., 34.

51   Tim Berners-Lee, telephone interview with the author, August 28, 2008.

51   Berners-Lee with Fischetti, 31.

55   Jim Wayne, "Tim Berners-Lee Web of people," *Knight Digital Media Center*, December 4, 2007. http://www.ojr.org/ojr/stories/071204wayne (January 10, 2008).

58   Mark Ward, "How the Web Went World Wide," *BBC News*, Augusts 3, 2006. http://news.bbc.co.uk/1/hi/technology/5242252.stm (January 10, 2008).

58   Berners-Lee with Fischetti, 47.

59   Tim Berners-Lee, telephone interview with the author, January 16, 2008.

60   Gillies and Cailliau, 219.

63   Berners-Lee with Fischetti, 59.

65   Ibid., 66.

68   Ibid., 76.

69 Ibid., 73.

70 Ibid., 74.

75 Gillies and Cailliau, 267.

73 Ibid., 266.

73 Ibid.

74 Nathan Halverson, "Filling the Do-It-Yourself Niche," interviewed by Dale Dougherty, *Press Democrat*, May 7, 2007, http://www1.pressdemocrat .com/apps/pbsc.dll/article?AID=/20070507/NEWS/705070310/1074/ BUSINESS09 (August 9, 2008).

75 Berners-Lee with Fischetti, 86.

76 Gillies and Cailliau, 281.

78 Tim Berners-Lee, telephone interview with the author, August 28, 2008.

80 Apple Computer, "The Home Computer That's Ready to Work, Play and Grow with You," *Scientific American*, September 1977, available online at http://home.swbell.net/rubywand/R001a2ad.htm (September 21, 2008).

80 Berners-Lee with Fischetti, 101.

82 Innovations Report, "World Wide Web Consortium to Move European Host to ERCIM. INRIA Instrumental in Bringing Two International Initiatives Together," *Innovations Report,* November 27, 2002, http:// www.innovations-report.de/html/berichte/informationstechnologie/ bericht-14802.html (November 19, 2008).

84 Berners-Lee with Fischetti, 115.

85 Ibid., 112.

86 Ibid., 115.

86 Ibid.

87 Andy Carvin, "DDN Articles: Tim Berners-Lee: Weaving a Semantic Web," *Digital Divide Network*, February 1, 2005, http://www .digitaldivide.net/articles/view.php?ArticleID=20 (January 10, 2008).

90 Berners-Lee with Fischetti, 165.

90 Tim Berners-Lee, November 2008.

92 Tim Berners-Lee, telephone interview with the author, August 28, 2008.

93 Wright, "The Man Who Invented the Web."

94 James Adlam, "Profile: Father of the Web's Fondness for Sheen," *Richmond and Twickenham Times*, January 22, 2004, http://www. richmondandtwickenhamtimes.co.uk/news/452142.0/ (August 7, 2007).

94　BBC News, "Creator of the Web Turns Knight," *BBC News*, July 16, 2004, http://news.bbc.co.uk/1/hi/technologoy/3899723.stm (July 5, 2007).

95　Simon Winchester, "Tim Berners-Lee, OE; inventor of the World Wide Web," *Emanuel School*, n.d., http://www.emanuel.org.uk/oldemanuels/bernerslee.htm (July 12, 2007).

95　Tim Berners-Lee, interview with the author, January 16, 2008.

96　Timothy Berners-Lee, Testimony, CSAIL Decentralized Information Group, Massachusetts Institute of Technology before the United States House of Representatives, Committee on Telecommunications and the Internet Hearing on the "Digital Future of the United States: Part I—the Future of the World Wide Web," *Decentralized Information Group,* March 1, 2007, http://dig.csail.mit.edu/2007/03/01-ushouse-future-of-the-Web (January 10. 2008).

96　Ibid.

96　Tim Berners-Lee, telephone interview with the author, August 28, 2008.

96　Tim Berners-Lee, November 2008.

SELECTED BIBLIOGRAPHY

Books

Berners-Lee, Tim. *Weaving the Web: The Original Design and Ultimate Destiny of the World Wide Web*. With Mark Fischetti. New York: HarperBusiness, 2000.

Gillies, James, and Robert Cailliau. *How the Web Was Born: The Story of the World Wide Web*. Oxford, NY: Oxford University Press, 2000.

Hafner, Katie and Matthew Lyon. *Where Wizards Stay Up Late: The Origins of the Internet*. New York: Simon & Schuster, 1996.

Articles and Internet Sources

Academy of Achievement. "Interview: Timothy Berners-Lee, Father of the World Wide Web." *Academy of Achievement*. June 22, 2007. http://www.achievement.org/autodoc/printmember/ber1int-1 (July 15, 2008).

Adlam, James. "Profile: Father of Web's fondness for Sheen." *Richmond and Twickenham Times*. January 22, 2004. http://www.richmondandtwickenhamtimes.co.uk/news/452142.0/ (August 7, 2007).

BBC News. "Web Inventor Is 'Greatest Inventor.'" *BBC News*. January 28, 2005. http://news.bbc.co.uk/1/hi/uk/4214473.stm (July 5, 2007).

Berners-Lee, Tim. "Answers for Young People." *World Wide Web Consortium*. N.d. http://www.w3.org/People/Berners-Lee/Kids (January 16, 2009).

———. "Sir Timothy Berners-Lee KBE, FRS, FREng, FRSA: Longer Biography." *WorldWide Web Consortium*. N.d. http://www.w3.org/People/Berners-Lee/Longer.html (January 16, 2009).

———. "The World Wide Web—Past, Present and Future." *Journal of Digital Information*, 1, no. 1, July 17, 1996. http://jodi.tamu.edu/Articles/v01/i01/Berners-Lee/ (January 10, 2008).

Farndale, Nigel. "Tim Berners-Lee: A Very British Boffin." *Telegraph.co.uk*. March 30, 2008. http://www.telegraph.co.uk/connected/main/jhtml?xml=/connected/2008/03/30/sv_timbernerslee.xml&page=2 (July 15, 2008).

Johnson, Bobbie. "The Guardian Profile: Tim Berners-Lee." *Guardian*. August 12, 2005. http://www.guardian.co.uk/uk_news/story/0,,1547428,00.html (July 5, 2007).

Kroeker, Kirk L. "Tim Berners-Lee Wins Finnish 'Nobel' Prize." *Technology News.* April 15, 2004. http://www.technewsworld.com/story/ networking/33447.html (July 20, 2007).

Martinson, Jane. "The Man Who Made the Web." *Guardian Unlimited.* November 24, 1999. http://www.guardian.co.uk/technology/1999/ nov/24/internet.guardianweekly (January 16, 2009).

Morris, Richard. "Tim Berners-Lee, Geek of the Week," *Simple-talk.com.* June 20, 2008. http://www.simple-talk.com/content/print.aspx?article=521 (July 15, 2008).

Newsmaker Q&A. "The Web's Weaver Looks Forward." *BusinessWeek.* March 27, 2002. http://www.businessweek.com/bwdaily/dnflash/mar2002/ nf20020327_4579.htm (February 7, 2008).

News Office. "Tim Berners-Lee, Inventor of the World Wide Web, Knighted by Queen Elizabeth II." *Massachusetts Institute of Technology.* July 16, 2004. http://Web.mit.edu/newsoffice/2004/berners-lee-knighted.html (July 12, 2007).

Quittner, Joshua. "The Time 100: Scientists and Thinkers: Tim Berners-Lee." *Time,* March 29, 1999. http://www.time.com/time/time100/scientist/ profile/bernerslee03.html (July 5, 2007).

Royal Society. "Professor Tim Berners-Lee FRS—Weaver of the Web." *Royal Society.* N.d. http://royalsociety.org/page.asp?tip=1&id=1482 (January 10, 2008).

Stewart, William. "Tim Berners-Lee, Robert Cailliau, and the World Wide Web." *LivingInternet.com.* 1996. http://www.livinginternet.com/w/ wi_lee.htm (July 12, 2007).

Tim Berners-Lee. Interviewed by Daniel Morrow. "Tim Berners-Lee Oral History." Computerworld Honors Program International Archives. Edited transcript of a video history interview. April 23, 2001. available online at http://www.cwhonors.org/search/oral_history_archive/tim_berners_lee/ Berners-Lee.pdf. Cambridge, MA

Time. "Tim Berners-Lee: World Wide Web Inventor." *Time.com.* September 29, 1999. http://www.time.com/time/community/ transcripts/1999/092999berners-lee.html (January 16, 2009).

Ward, Mark. "How the Web Went World Wide." *BBC News.* August 3, 2006. http://news.bbc.co.uk/1/hi/technology/5242252.stm (January 10, 2008).

Wayne, Jim. "Tim Berners-Lee's Web of People." *Knight Digital Media Center.* December 4, 2007. http://www.ojr.org/ojr/stories/071204wayne/ (January 16, 2009).

Winchester, Simon. "Tim Berners-Lee, OE: Inventor of the World Wide Web." *Emanuel School.* N.d. http://www.emanuel.org.uk/oldemanuels/ bernerslee.htm (July 12, 2007).

Wright, Robert. "The Man Who Invented the Web: Tim Berners-Lee Started a Revolution, but It Didn't Go Exactly as Planned." *Time*, May 19, 1997. http://www.chuckallan.com/fccj/cgs2555/tim-berners-lee.html (July 5, 2007).

Interviews

Berners-Lee, Tim. Telephone interviews with author. January 16, 2008; August 28, 2008.

Daly, Janet, former head of communiations for W3C. Telephone conversations with author. August 5, 2008; August 28, 2008.

FURTHER READING AND WEBSITES

Books

Amihud, Zohar. *Look Mom! I Built My Own Web Site.* 4th ed. Fords, NJ: BookChamp, 2005.

Gaines, Ann. *Tim Berners-Lee and the Development of the World Wide Web.* Hockessin, DE: Mitchell Lane Publishers, 2002.

Lesinski, Jeanne M. *Bill Gates.* Minneapolis: Twenty-First Century Books, 2009.

McPherson, Stephanie Sammartino. *Ordinary Genius.* Minneapolis: Twenty-First Century Books, 1995.

——. *Stephen Hawking.* Minneapolis: Twenty-First Century Books, 2007.

Selfridge, Benjamin, and Peter Selfridge. *A Kid's Guide to Creating Web Pages for Home and School.* Chicago: Zephyr Press, 2004.

Sherman, Josepha. *History of the Internet.* New York: Watts Library, Turtleback, 2003.

Stewart, Melissa. *Tim Berners-Lee: Inventor of the World Wide Web.* Ferguson Career Biographies series. New York: Chelsea House, 2001.

Woods, Michael, and Mary B. Woods. *The History of Communication.* Minneapolis: Lerner Publications Company, 2006.

Websites

Answers for Young People: Tim Berners-Lee
http://www.3org/People/Berners -Lee/kids.html
Tim Berners-Lee answers some questions frequently asked by children such as "What made you think of the WWW?" and "What happens when I click on a link?"

CERN: Where the Web Was Born
http://public.Web.cern/ch/Public/en/About/Web-en.html
This website presents a brief history of the World Wide Web and a simple explanation of the way the Web works.

Extraordinary People: Tim Berners-Lee
http://express.howstuffworks. com/ep-berners-lee.htm
This brief introduction to Tim Berners-Lee includes simple definitions of terms such as microprocessor, hypertext, URL, and browser.

Internet Pioneers: Tim Berners-Lee
http://www.ibiblio.org/pioneers/lee.html
This short history of the Web follows Tim Berners-Lee from his early days at CERN through the creation of the World Wide Web Consortium.

Welcome to Info.cern.ch
http://info.cern.ch/
The "world's first-ever Web server" presents a brief history of the World Wide Web.

PHOTO ACKNOWLEDGMENTS

The additional images in this book are used with the permission of: AP Photo/Elise Amendola, p. 1; © Carlos Alvarez/Getty Images, p. 3; AP Photo/ Jim Rogash, p. 4; © Manchester University, p. 6; © Topham/The Image Works, p. 8; © Niall McDiarmid/Alamy, p. 11; © Time & Life Pictures/Getty Images, p. 12; © Peter Titmuss/Alamy, p. 14; © SSPL/The Image Works, pp. 17, 21 (bottom left), 41; © SuperStock, Inc./SuperStock, p. 20; © Hulton Archive/Getty Images, p. 21 (top left); © Tom Munnecke/Hulton Archive/ Getty Images, p. 21 (top right); © Dan Ford Connolly/Time & Life Pictures/ Getty Images, p. 21 (bottom right); © Johannes Simon/Getty Images, p. 22; © iStockphoto.com/Andrey Prokhorov, p. 24; © Laura Westlund/Independent Picture Service, pp. 25, 49; © Tom Merton/Digital Vision/Getty Images, pp. 30, 57, 61, 62, 67 (top), 83, 88, 91; AP Photo/Reed Saxon, p. 36; AP Photo/ Charles Dharapak, p. 37 (top left); AP Photo/fls, p. 37 (bottom right); © CERN/ SSPL/The Image Works, pp. 38, 43, 52; © Pallava Bagla/CORBIS, pp. 46, 54; AP Photo/Erik S. Lesser, p. 50; AP Photo/Paul Sakuma, p. 56; © CERN, pp. 58, 68; © D.C. Lowe/SuperStock, p. 64; © Cindy Charles/Liaison/Getty Images, p. 67 (bottom); © Peter Richardson/Robert Harding World Imagery/Getty Images, p. 72; REUTERS/Steffen Schmidt, p. 77; © Stan Honda/AFP/Getty Images, p. 78; AP Photo/Stephan Savoia, p. 79; © Gaillard/AFP/Getty Images, p. 81; © Michael L. Abramson/Time & Life Pictures/Getty Images, p. 84; © Andrew Brusso/CORBIS, p. 87; AP Photo, p. 93; © Martti Kainulainen/AFP/Getty Images, p. 95.

Front Cover: AP Photo/Mike Groll.

ABOUT THE AUTHOR

Stephanie Sammartino McPherson, a former journalist, enjoys writing about science for young people. Her children's books include *Ordinary Genius: The Story of Albert Einstein*, *Jonas Salk: Conquering Polio*, and *Wilbur and Orville Wright: Taking Flight* (written with her nephew Joseph Sammartino Gardner) as well as a biography of Stephen Hawking. McPherson and her husband, Richard, live in Virginia but also call California home. They are the parents of two grown children.

ACKNOWLEDGMENTS

First and foremost, a very big thank-you to Sir Timothy Berners-Lee for sharing his story and reviewing this manuscript. Thanks also to Janet Daly for her helpful insights and comments, to Amy van der Hiel for coordinating phone calls; to Karen Chernyaev for her expert editorial advice and suggestions; to my husband, Richard, for reading the manuscript and helping with diagrams. I also appreciate the comments of other family members who read this manuscript: Angelo and Marion Sammartino, Jennifer McPherson, Marianne McPherson, Joseph Gardner, and Jonathan Gardner.